KetoFasty

Cookbook

The Newest and Most Effective Recipes for Intermittent Fasting and Timed Ketogenic Meals, Discover the Advantages of KetoFasty on Your Body, Mind and Soul Wellness

By

Dr. Stephanie Ramos,

Dr. Joseph Evans & Dr. William Moore

About the Authors

Dr. Stephanie Ramos *is a practicing chef who works significantly to improve the overall dietary standards of the people. Her area of expertise includes several regional and exotic cuisines. Moreover, she has been successful in devising various dietary plans for weight loss. Her concerns for obesity and related health disorders remained the pivot of her various researches. It is this in-depth study which led to a progressive tilt towards creating hundreds of delightful yet healthy meals.*

Dr. JosephEvans *is largely associated with the Ketogenic dietary approach because of his extensive work on the diet. For years, he has been studying the Ketogenic diet and its impact on the human mind and body. He has written several articles on the importance of the ketogenic diet and prescribed several ways for its successful incorporation. Through his work, he has bridged public understanding of the ketogenic food to the diet itself. His contribution to this book has added a much detailed account on the Ketogenic lifestyle.*

Dr. William Moore is known for his deep analysis and research in the field of fasting. He has been actively engaged in highlighting the importance of intermittent fasting as a successful health approach. According to him sufficient gaps between meal intake can better harness nutrients and calories and prepare the body well for active metabolism. He has presented similar views over the text of this book and successfully linked the benefits of cyclic intermittent fasting with that of the ketogenic diet to come up with the idea of KetoFasty.

Independently working in their respective fields, all three experts always wanted to take their dietary approaches to the next level where they could make the most impact. Dr. Evans, therefore, reached out to Dr. Moore and floated the idea of working together on different variations of ketogenic diet plans. It is when they came up with the idea of fusing it with intermittent fasting and to create a whole new combination of diet in itself. To make the content more useful in a practical sense, Dr. Stephanie Ramos stepped in and offered her years of experience as a chef. It was her contributions which turned the diet into reality and together all these authors created a series of two books, covering the idea of KetoFasty at length.

Contents

Introduction

If you are reading this book, you must be very well familiar with the idea of a ketogenic diet plan. If not, you may have a basic understanding of this uniquely healthy dietary approach. For the sake of a reminder, there shall be a quick flashback into all the Keto specific details, but more precisely the connection between Ketogenic food with intermittent fasting will be established in this book. Conventional Keto plan calls for certain restrictions on the carb-rich food and pushes you to a high-fat dietary approach. A well-followed Keto diet plan is enough to procure all of the various health benefits, and when paired with fasting, it guarantees even better effects over mind and body. This cookbook will, however, be highlighting more of the practical angle of this dietary approach, as most of its sections are comprised of a variety of KetoFasty related recipes. It is such a guideline which could serve its purpose right in the kitchen. With so many of the recipes, this book can assist well in adopting the right pace for the KetoFasty diet plan. Let's have a quick flash back of all the things we know about the Ketogenic diet and a KetoFasty.

Conventional Ketogenic Diet

By convention, the Ketogenic diet is famous for its low carb approach. It says to omit all the direct sources of the sugars and carbohydrates from the routine diet and emphasizes more on the fat intake. There is no single prewritten formula for it; we need to be more cautious along the way while keeping following few important points in mind:

1. Each meal should not have the carb-content greater than 11-13 grams.
2. All the natural sugars and sweeteners have to be avoided.
3. Vegetables rich in starch such as yams and potatoes should not be used.
4. Fat rich ingredients should be used in a greater amount.
5. Avoid animal milk and switch to almond or coconut milk.
6. Substitute the high carb content with low carb and high-fat ingredients.

KetoFasty

KetoFasty is more than a diet; it is a lifestyle or a combination of steps that need to be taken to achieve great health benefits in a short period of time. Unlike conventional ketogenic diet plan, this one, in particular, is characterized by the periods of fasting in between the two ketogenic meals. The pattern of fasting depends entirely on the person. There are several approaches to intermittent fasting which includes a complete 24 hours fast in a week, or 5:2, alternate fasting, etc. Which ever pattern suits a person's existing routine can be considered most suitable. However, each period of fasting should be started from a ketogenic meal and ends on a ketogenic food. This means you cannot take sugary juices or market bought drinks, sweets or carb-rich bread or cakes before and after each fast. These meals should have more cheeses, oils, meat, creams, etc and lesser grains, lentils or pulses. In short, KetoFasty helps manage both the schedule and the menu for the table. It combines the time and material together at one place which greatly benefits people having heart conditions, diabetes, neural issues, obesity, and poor metabolism.

Why Switch to KetoFasty?

Firstly, KetoFasty helps everyone against the looming threats of weight gain or obesity. Even when a person suffers from serious obesity, this dietary approach helps to lose a couple of pounds just in days. Mere fasting can never prove to be effective in that regard, as a person can end eating more at the end of the fast than the bodily requirements. KetoFasty, however, sets a limit on this intake and helps by initiating ketosis in the body. Fats are actively broken down during the fast and toxins are released out of the body.

Reducing the oxidative stress in the body is another great benefit of this diet. In other words, it helps remove all the agents from the body which would otherwise cause oxidation. Ketosis is the phenomenon of importance in this regard. By avoid direct energy sources like carbohydrates and leaning more on fats for energy consumption, we simply reduce the intake of the oxidative agents. While the fats are metabolized, these agents are expelled out of the body.

Both fasting and ketogenic diet helps nourish the brain cells. Therefore, KetoFasty is one of the great methods to strengthen the mind and make it resistant to many psychological disorders. Similarly, KetoFasty is also effective to deal with any of the cardiac diseases or other related conditions. It is also a source of keeping the sugar levels balanced in the blood. Such a fast is quite effective for diabetic patients who cannot otherwise afford the risks of fasting. Through this approach, they can to keep their glucose levels in check.

Smoothie Recipes

Strawberry Smoothie

A super healthy smoothie of strawberries... This smoothie is loaded with the healthy touch of chia seeds and almonds with a distinctly sweet taste of strawberries.

Yield: 2 servings

Preparation time: 10 minutes

Allergens: nuts

Ingredients:

- 1¼ cups frozen strawberries

- 2 tablespoons almonds, chopped
- ¼ teaspoon ground cinnamon
- 5-6 drops liquid stevia
- 1¾cups unsweetened almond milk

Instructions:

1. In a high-speed blender, pulse all the ingredients until smooth.
2. Pour the smoothie into serving glasses and serve.

Nutritional Information per Serving
Calories: 84
Fat: 4.6g
Sat Fat: 0.4g
Cholesterol: 0mg
Sodium: 158mg
Carbohydrates: 10.8g
Fiber: 3.3g
Sugar: 5.7g
Protein: 1.5g

Blackberry & Lettuce Smoothie

Treat your body with one of delicious and healthy smoothie... Blackberries make a nice combo with whipping cream, cream cheese, and coconut oil.

Yield: 2 servings

Preparation time: 10 minutes

Allergens: dairy

Ingredients:

- 1¼ cups fresh blackberries
- ½ cup heavy whipping cream
- ½ cup cream cheese, softened
- ½ tablespoon coconut oil
- 3-5 drops liquid stevia
- 1 cup chilled water

Instructions:

1. In a blender, process all the ingredients until smooth.
2. Pour the smoothie into serving glasses and serve.

Nutritional Information per Serving

Calories: 374

Fat: 35.2g

Sat Fat: 226g

Cholesterol: 105mg

Sodium: 184mg

Carbohydrates: 11g

Fiber: 4.8g

Sugar: 4.5g

Protein: 6.3g

Blueberry Smoothie

A breakfast smoothie with one of the healthy fruits... The combo of blueberries and lettuce compliments almond milk nicely.

Yield: 2 servings

Preparation time: 10 minutes

Allergens: dairy

Ingredients:

- ¾ cup fresh blueberries
- 1½ cups romaine lettuce, chopped
- 4-6 drops liquid stevia
- 1½ unsweetened almond milk

Instructions:

1. In a blender, process all the ingredients until smooth.
2. Pour the smoothie into serving glasses and serve.

Nutritional Information per Serving
Calories: 67

Fat: 2.9g
Sat Fat: 0.2g
Cholesterol: 0mg
Sodium: 138mg
Carbohydrates: 10g
Fiber: 2.3g
Sugar: 5.8g
Protein: 1.4g

Mixed Berries Smoothie

A healthy combo of mixed berries, coconut and cottage cheese with coconut water... Fresh coconut water adds a delish taste in this smoothie.

Yield: 2 servings

Preparation time: 10 minutes

Allergens: dairy, nuts

Ingredients:

- ½ cups fresh strawberries
- ½ cup fresh blueberries
- 1 tablespoon unsweetened coconut, shredded
- 1-2 packets stevia powder
- 1/3 cup cottage cheese
- 1½ cups unsweetened almond milk

Instructions:

1. In a blender, process all the ingredients until smooth.
2. Pour the smoothie into serving glasses and serve.

Nutritional Information per Serving

Calories: 105

Fat: 4.4g

Sat Fat: 1.5g

Cholesterol: 3mg

Sodium: 289mg

Carbohydrates: 10g

Fiber: 2.6g

Sugar: 5.6g

Protein: 6.5g

Vanilla Smoothie

A classically delicious treat that satisfies healthy minds...
This classic smoothie is packed with protein-rich
ingredients.

Yield: 2 servings

Preparation time: 10 minutes

Allergens: nuts

Ingredients:

- ½ cup unsweetened vanilla whey protein powder
- 4 tablespoons almond butter
- 2 teaspoons organic vanilla extract
- 6-8 drops liquid stevia
- 2 cups unsweetened almond milk

Instructions:

1. In a blender, process all the ingredients until smooth.
2. Pour the smoothie into serving glasses and serve.

Nutritional Information per Serving

Calories: 355

Fat: 22.7g

Sat Fat: 2g

Cholesterol: 24mg

Sodium: 200mg

Carbohydrates: 10g

Fiber: 4.2g

Sugar: 3.2g

Protein: 29.8g

Mocha Smoothie

One of the favorite and super delicious smoothies for chocolate lovers... This creamy, frothy and frosty smoothie will boost up your metabolism nicely.

Yield: 2 servings

Preparation time: 10 minutes

Allergens: dairy, nuts

Ingredients:

- 2 teaspoons instant espresso powder
- 2-3 tablespoons Swerve
- 2 teaspoons cacao powder
- ½ cup plain Greek yogurt
- 1 cup unsweetened almond milk

Instructions:

1. In a blender, process all the ingredients until smooth.
2. Pour the smoothie into serving glasses and serve.

Nutritional Information per Serving

Calories: 73

Fat: 2.8g

Sat Fat: 1g

Cholesterol: 4mg

Sodium: 137mg

Carbohydrates: 8.2g

Fiber: 1g

Sugar: 4.3g

Protein: 4.3g

Cucumber Smoothie

A green breakfast smoothie that is refreshing and healthy as well... The adding of lemon juice adds a refreshing ouch in this smoothie.

Yield: 2 servings

Preparation time: 10 minutes

Allergens: absent

Ingredients:

- 1 small cucumber, peeled and chopped
- 1 cup mixed fresh greens (spinach, kale, beet greens), trimmed and chopped
- ½ cup lettuce, torn
- 2 tablespoons fresh parsley leaves
- 2 tablespoons fresh mint leaves
- 6-8 drops liquid stevia
- 1 teaspoon fresh lemon juice
- 1½ cups water

Instructions:

1. In a blender, process all the ingredients until smooth.
2. Pour the smoothie into serving glasses and serve.

Nutritional Information per Serving

Calories: 31

Fat: 0.3g

Sat Fat: 0.1g

Cholesterol: 0mg

Sodium: 30mg

Carbohydrates: 7g

Fiber: 1.6g

Sugar: 2.7g

Protein: 1.6g

Avocado Smoothie

A super nutritious and delicious smoothie of avocado...
Avocado adds an amazing amount of creaminess in this
smoothie.

Yield: 2 servings

Preparation time: 10 minutes

Allergens: nuts

Ingredients:

- ½ large avocado, peeled, pitted and chopped
  roughly
- 2 cups fresh spinach
- 1 tablespoon MCT oil
- 1 teaspoon organic vanilla extract
- 6-8 drops liquid stevia
- 1½ cups unsweetened almond milk

Instructions:

1. In a blender, process all the ingredients until
   smooth.

2. Pour the smoothie into serving glasses and serve.

Nutritional Information per Serving

Calories: 195

Fat: 19.6g

Sat Fat: 9.3g

Cholesterol: 0mg

Sodium: 162mg

Carbohydrates: 7.2g

Fiber: 4.8g

Sugar: 0.7g

Protein: 2.6g

Green Strawberry Smoothie

A power packed and tasty breakfast smoothie for all family... This mildly sweet smoothie is packed with the goodness of fresh greens and strawberries.

Yield: 2 servings

Preparation time: 10 minutes

Allergens: nuts

Ingredients:

- ½ cup fresh strawberries, hulled and sliced
- 1cup fresh kale, trimmed and chopped
- 1 cup fresh spinach, chopped
- ½ cucumber, peeled and chopped
- 4-6 drops liquid stevia
- 1½ cups unsweetened almond milk
- ¼ cup ice cubes

Instructions:

1. In a blender, process all the ingredients until smooth.
2. Pour the smoothie into serving glasses and serve.

Nutritional Information per Serving

Calories: 73

Fat: 2.6g

Sat Fat: 0.3g

Cholesterol: 0mg

Sodium: 164mg

Carbohydrates: 11g

Fiber: 2.7g

Sugar: 3.1g

Protein: 2.9g

Greens Smoothie

A smoothie with healthy benefits of strawberries and fresh spinach... Fresh ginger and parsley compliments berries and spinach nicely.

Yield: 2 servings

Preparation time: 10 minutes

Allergens: absent

Ingredients:

- 2 cups romaine lettuce, chopped
- 1 cup fresh baby spinach
- 1 cup fresh baby kale, tough ribs removed
- ¼ cup fresh mint leaves
- 2 tablespoons fresh lemon juice
- 8-10 drops liquid stevia
- 1½ cups filtered water

Instructions:

1. In a blender, process all the ingredients until smooth.
2. Pour the smoothie into serving glasses and serve.

Nutritional Information per Serving

Calories: 36

Fat: 0.4g

Sat Fat: 0.2g

Cholesterol: 0mg

Sodium: 36mg

Carbohydrates: 7g

Fiber: 2g

Sugar: 0.9g

Protein: 2.2g

Red Smoothie

A smoothie with a bright and beautiful red color...
Combination of red veggies and berries make a healthy
smoothie.

Yield: 2 servings

Preparation time: 10 minutes

Allergens: absent

Ingredients:

- ½ cup fresh raspberries
- ½ fresh strawberries
- ½ red bell pepper, seeded and chopped
- ½ cup red cabbage, chopped
- 1 small tomato
- 1 cup filtered water

Instructions

1. In a blender, process all the ingredients until smooth.
2. Pour the smoothie into serving glasses and serve.

Nutritional Information per Serving

Calories: 39

Fat: 0.4g

Sat Fat: 0g

Cholesterol: 0mg

Sodium: 6mg

Carbohydrates: 8g

Fiber: 3.5g

Sugar: 4.8g

Protein: 1.3g

Pumpkin Smoothie

A simple and best way to enjoy the fall season in a glass of smoothie... This delectable smoothie is packed with healthy nutrients.

Yield: 2 servings

Preparation time: 10 minutes

Allergens: dairy, nuts

Ingredients:

- ½ cup homemade pumpkin puree
- 1 scoop unsweetened whey protein powder
- ¾ teaspoon pumpkin pie spice
- 2 teaspoons Erythritol
- 1 tablespoon coconut oil
- ½ cup sour cream
- 1 cup unsweetened almond milk

Instructions:

1. In a blender, process all the ingredients until smooth.

2. Pour the smoothie into serving glasses and serve.

Nutritional Information per Serving

Calories: 278

Fat: 21.5g

Sat Fat: 13.8g

Cholesterol: 38mg

Sodium: 150mg

Carbohydrates: 9g

Fiber: 2.4g

Sugar: 2.8g

Protein: 14.1g

Breakfast Recipes

Chocolaty Nuts Granola

A super healthy, delicious and comforting breakfast treat for the whole family... Especially your toddlers would love to enjoy this chocolaty and nutty granola.

Yield: 12 servings

Preparation time: 15 minutes

Cooking time: 18 minutes

Allergens: nuts, dairy

Ingredients:

- 1½ cups almonds
- 1½ cups hazelnuts
- ¼ cup cacao powder
- 1 cup flax seeds meal
- Pinch of sea salt
- ¼ cup unsalted butter, melted
- ¼ cup almond butter, melted
- 2 ounces unsweetened dark chocolate, chopped
- 1/3 cup Erythritol
- 20 drops stevia extract

Instructions:

1. Preheat your oven to 300° F (150° C). Line a large baking sheet.
2. Add the nuts in a food processor and pulse until coarse crumbs form.
3. Place the nut mixture into a bowl.
4. Add he cacao powder, flax seeds meal and salt and mix until well combined.
5. In a pan, add the hazelnut oil, butter, and chocolate over low heat and cook for about 2-3 minutes or until smooth, stirring continuously.
6. Stir in the Erythritol and immediately, remove from the heat.
7. Add the butter mixture over nut mixture and toss to coat well.
8. Transfer the mixture onto prepared baking sheet evenly.
9. Bake for about 15 minutes, stirring after every 5 minutes.
10. Turn off the oven but keep the baking sheet in oven for about 20 minutes, stirring occasionally.
11. Remove the baking sheet from the oven and let the granola cool completely before serving.
12. This granola can be preserved in an airtight container.

Nutritional Information per Serving

Calories: 255

Fat: 21.4g

Sat Fat: 4.9g

Cholesterol: 11mg

Sodium: 51mg

Carbohydrates: 11g

Fiber: 6.2g

Sugar: 3.4g

Protein: 7.4g

Creamy Porridge

Start your day with this warming and delicious porridge...This creamy porridge is perfect for a warm and hearty breakfast.

Yield: 4 servings

Preparation time: 10 minutes

Cooking time: 7 minutes

Allergens: egg, dairy, nuts

Ingredients:

- 1½ cups water
- 1/3 cup almond flour
- 2 tablespoons flax meal
- Pinch of salt
- 2 organic eggs, beaten
- 2 tablespoons heavy cream
- 2 tablespoons Erythritol
- 4 teaspoons unsalted butter
- 3 tablespoons fresh blueberries

Instructions:

1. In a pan, add the water, almond flour, ground flax and salt over medium-high heat and bring to a boil, stirring continuously.
2. Now, reduce the heat to medium and cook for about 2-3 minutes, beating continuously.
3. Remove from heat and slowly, add the beaten eggs, beating eggs continuously.
4. Return the pan over medium heat and cook for about 2-3 minutes or until mixture becomes thick.
5. Remove from heat and beat for at least 30 seconds.
6. Add the heavy cream, Erythritol, and butter and beat until well combined.
7. Serve hot with the topping of berries.

Nutritional Information per Serving

Calories: 166

Fat: 14.6g

Sat Fat: 5.2g

Cholesterol: 102mg

Sodium: 119mg

Carbohydrates: 11.3g

Fiber: 2.2g

Sugar: 1.2g

Protein: 5.8g

Yogurt Waffles

Surprisingly delicious and satisfying waffles for breakfast...
Eggs, butter, yogurt, almond milk, and whey protein
powder team up greatly for these waffles.

Yield: 5 servings

Preparation time: 15 minutes

Cooking time: 25 minutes

Allergens: egg, dairy, nuts

Ingredients:

- ½ cup golden flax seeds meal
- ½ cup plus 3 tablespoons almond flour
- 1-1½ tablespoons Erythritol
- 1 tablespoon unsweetened vanilla whey protein powder
- ¼ teaspoon baking soda
- ½ teaspoon organic baking powder
- ¼ teaspoon xanthan gum
- Salt, to taste
- 1 large organic egg, white and yolk separated
- 1 organic whole egg
- 2 tablespoons unsweetened almond milk
- 1½ tablespoons unsalted butter
- 3 ounces plain Greek yogurt
- ¼ cup fresh strawberries, hulled and sliced

Instructions:

1. Preheat the waffle iron and then grease it.
2. In a large bowl, add the flour, Erythritol, protein powder, baking soda, baking powder, xanthan gum, and salt and mix until well combined.
3. In a second small bowl, add the egg white and beat until stiff peaks form.

49

4. In a third bowl, add 2 egg yolk, whole egg, almond milk, butter, and yogurt and beat until well combined.
5. Add the egg mixture into flour mixture and mix until well combined.
6. Gently, fold in the beaten egg whites
7. Place ¼ cup of the mixture into preheated waffle iron and cook for about 4-5 minutes or until golden brown.
8. Repeat with the remaining mixture.
9. Serve warm with the topping of strawberries.

Nutritional Information per Serving

Calories: 243

Fat: 18.3g

Sat Fat: 4.1g

Cholesterol: 86mg

Sodium: 169mg

Carbohydrates: 10.2g

Fiber: 5.7g

Sugar: 2.3g

Protein: 11g

Cheese Crepes

A super easy and quick recipe for moist and yummy crepes... Parmesan and cream cheese adds moistness and extra flavoring to creeps.

Yield: 5 servings

Preparation time: 15 minutes

Cooking time: 20 minutes

Allergens: egg, dairy

Ingredients:

- 6 ounces cream cheese, softened
- 1/3 cup Parmesan cheese, grated
- 6 large organic eggs
- 1 teaspoon Erythritol
- 1½tablespoons coconut flour
- 1/8 teaspoon xanthan gum
- 2 tablespoons unsalted butter

Instructions:

1. In a blender, add the cream cheese, Parmesan cheese, eggs and Erythritol and pulse on low speed until well combined.
2. While the motor is running, place the coconut flour and xanthan gum and pulse until a thick mixture is formed.
3. Now, pulse on medium speed for about 5-10 seconds.
4. Transfer the mixture into a bowl and set aside for at least 5 minutes.
5. In a nonstick frying pan, melt the butter over medium-low heat.
6. Add ¼ cup of the mixture and tilt the pan to spread into a thin layer.
7. Cook for about 1½ minutes or until the edges become brown.
8. Carefully, flip the crepe and cook for about 15-20 seconds more.
9. Repeat with the remaining mixture.
10. Serve warm with your favorite keto friendly filling.

Nutritional Information per Serving
Calories: 283
Fat: 24.3g
Sat Fat: 13.5g
Cholesterol: 200mg

Sodium: 274mg
Carbohydrates: 3.8g
Fiber: 1.6g
Sugar: 0.8g
Protein: 12.9g

Blueberry Pancakes

A hit recipe for those days when fresh blueberries are in season... These light, fluffy and fruity pancakes are a classic choice for breakfast.

Yield: 3 servings

Preparation time: 15 minutes

Cooking time: 21 minutes

Allergens: egg, nuts

Ingredients:

- ½ cup almond flour
- 2 tablespoons coconut flour
- ½ teaspoon organic baking powder
- 1 teaspoon ground cinnamon
- 1½ tablespoons Erythritol
- ¼ cup unsweetened almond milk
- 3 large organic eggs
- ¼ cup fresh blueberries

Instructions:

1. In a high-speed blender, add all ingredients pulse until a thick mixture is formed.
2. Place the mixture into a bowl and gently, fold in blueberries.
3. Set aside for about 5-10 minutes.
4. Heat a lightly greased skillet over medium-low heat.
5. Add about ¼ cup of the mixture and with the back of a spatula, spread it into desired thickness.
6. Immediately, cover the skillet and cook for about 4 minutes.
7. Uncover and carefully, flip the side.
8. Cook for 3 minutes or until golden brown.
9. Repeat with the remaining mixture.
10. Serve warm.

Nutritional Information per Serving

Calories: 231

Fat: 12.7g

Sat Fat: 3.6g

Cholesterol: 186mg

Sodium: 106mg

Carbohydrates: 12g

Fiber: 6.1g

Sugar: 2.9g

Protein: 11.8g

Savory Broccoli Muffins

Try cheesy broccoli muffin for a savory but delish breakfast... These tasty and nutrient dense muffins will start your day in a perfect way.

Yield: 12 servings

Preparation time: 15 minutes

Cooking time: 20 minutes

Allergens: egg, dairy

Ingredients:

- 2 tablespoons unsalted butter
- 6 large organic eggs
- ½ cup heavy whipping cream
- ½ cup Parmesan cheese, grated
- Salt and ground black pepper, as required
- 1¼ cups broccoli, chopped
- 2 tablespoons fresh parsley, chopped
- ½ cup Swiss cheese, grated

Instructions:

1. Preheat your oven to 350° F (180° C). Grease 12 cups of a muffin tin.
2. In a bowl, add the eggs, cream, Parmesan cheese, salt, and black pepper and beat until well combined.
3. Divide the broccoli and parsley in the bottom of each prepared muffin cup evenly.
4. Top with the egg mixture, followed by the Swiss cheese.
5. Bake for about 20 minutes, rotating the pan once halfway through.
6. Remove from the oven and place onto a wire rack for about 5 minutes before serving.
7. Carefully, invert the muffins onto a serving platter and serve warm.

Nutritional Information per Serving
Calories: 103
Fat: 8.3g
Sat Fat: 4.4g
Cholesterol: 112mg
Sodium: 103mg
Carbohydrates: 1.2g
Fiber: 0.3g
Sugar: 0.4g
Protein: 6.1g

Flax Seeds Bread

One of the best homemade healthy bread with a soft texture... This incredible recipe of bread is great for beginners.

Yield: 12 servings

Preparation time: 15 minutes

Cooking time: 28 minutes

Allergens: egg, dairy

Ingredients:

- 2 cups flax seeds meal
- 2 tablespoons Swerve
- 1 tablespoon organic baking powder
- ½ teaspoon salt
- 5 organic eggs, beaten
- 5 tablespoons unsalted butter, melted
- ½ cup water
- 1 teaspoon organic vanilla extract

Instructions:

1. Preheat your oven to 350° F (180° C). Line a 15x10-inch loaf pan with a lightly, greased parchment paper.
2. In a bowl, add the flax seeds meal, Swerve, baking powder, and salt and mix.
3. In another bowl, add the eggs, butter, water and vanilla extract and beat until well combined.
4. Add the egg mixture into the bowl with flax seeds meal mixture and mix until well combined.
5. Place the mixture into prepared loaf pan.
6. Bake for about 24-28 minutes or until a toothpick inserted in the center comes out clean.
7. Remove the bread pan from oven and place onto a wire rack to cool for about 10 minutes.

8. Now, place the bread onto the wire rack to cool before slicing.
9. With a sharp knife, cut the bread loaf in desired sized slices and serve.

Nutritional Information per Serving

Calories: 196

Fat: 14.6g

Sat Fat: 4.5g

Cholesterol: 81mg

Sodium: 158mg

Carbohydrates: 9g

Fiber: 6.3g

Sugar: 0.2g

Protein: 7.7g

Pumpkin Bread

A unique layered bread for holiday morning breakfasts... This bread is packed with the flavors of pumpkin, cream cheese, and warm spices.

Yield: 16 servings

Preparation time: 20 minutes

Cooking time: 1 hour

Allergens: egg, dairy, nuts

Ingredients:

- 1 2/3 cups almond flour
- 1½ teaspoon organic baking powder
- ½teaspoon pumpkin pie spice
- ½teaspoon ground cinnamon
- ½teaspoon ground cloves
- ½teaspoon salt
- 8 ounces cream cheese, softened
- 6 organic egg, divided
- 1 tablespoon coconut flour
- 1 cup powdered Erythritol, divided
- 1teaspoon stevia extract powder, divided

- 1 teaspoon lemon extract
- 1 cup homemade pumpkin puree
- ½cup coconut oil, melted

Instructions:

1. Preheat your oven to 325° F (170° C). Lightly, grease 2 bread loaf pans.
2. In a bowl, add the almond flour, baking powder, spices and salt, and mix until well combined.
3. In a second bowl, add the cream cheese, 1 egg, coconut flour, ¼ cup of Erythritol and ¼ teaspoon of the stevia and with a wire whisk, beat until smooth.
4. In a third bowl, add the pumpkin puree, oil, 5 eggs, ¾ cup of the Erythritol and ¾ teaspoon of the stevia and with a wire whisk, beat until well combined.
5. Add the pumpkin mixture into the bowl of the flour mixture and mix until just combined.
6. Place about ¼ of the pumpkin mixture into each loaf pan evenly.
7. Top each pan with the cream cheese mixture evenly, followed by the remaining pumpkin mixture.

8. Bake for about 50-60 minutes or until a toothpick inserted in the center comes out clean.

9. Remove the bread pan from oven and place onto a wire rack to cool for about 10 minutes.

10. Now, invert the bread onto the wire rack to cool before slicing.

11. With a sharp knife, cut each bread loaf in the desired sized slices and serve.

Nutritional Information per Serving

Calories: 208

Fat: 19.4g

Sat Fat: 10.1g

Cholesterol: 77mg

Sodium: 142mg

Carbohydrates: 5.1g

Fiber: 2.1g

Sugar: 1.1g

Protein: 6g

Cheddar Scramble

A scramble that will be great for a Sunday morning family breakfast...This tasty recipe is a blend of scrambled eggs with cheddar cheese.

Yield: 6 servings

Preparation time: 10 minutes

Cooking time: 8 minutes

Allergens: egg, dairy

Ingredients:

- 2 tablespoons olive oil
- 1 jalapeño pepper, chopped
- 1 small yellow onion, chopped
- 12 large organic eggs, beaten lightly
- Salt and ground black pepper, as required
- 3 tablespoons fresh chives, chopped finely
- 4 ounces cheddar cheese, shredded

Instructions:

1. Heat oil in a large skillet over medium and sauté the jalapeño pepper and onion for about 4-5 minutes.
2. Add the eggs, salt, and black pepper and cook for about 3 minutes, stirring continuously.
3. Remove from the heat and immediately, stir in the chives and cheese.
4. Serve immediately.

Nutritional Information per Serving
Calories: 265
Fat: 20.9g
Sat Fat: 7.8g
Cholesterol: 390mg
Sodium: 285mg
Carbohydrates: 2.3g
Fiber: 0.4g
Sugar: 1.5g
Protein: 17.5g

Bacon & Cheddar Omelet

A great combination of cheese, eggs, and chives for a healthy breakfast... Surely this cheesy omelet will impress your family.

Yield: 2 servings

Preparation time: 10 minutes

Cooking time: 15 minutes

Allergens: egg, dairy

Ingredients:

- 4 large organic eggs
- 1 tablespoon fresh chives, minced
- Salt and ground black pepper, as required
- 4 bacon slices
- 1 tablespoon unsalted butter
- 2 ounces Cheddar cheese, shredded

Instructions:

1. In a bowl, add the eggs, chives, salt, and black pepper and beat until well combined.

2. Heat a non-stick frying pan over medium-high heat and cook the bacon slices for about 8-10 minutes.
3. Place the bacon onto a paper towel-lined plate to drain. Then chop the bacon slices.
4. With a paper towel, wipe out the frying pan.
5. In the same frying pan, melt the butter over medium-low heat and cook the egg mixture for about 2 minutes.
6. Carefully, flip the omelet and top with chopped bacon.
7. Cook for 1-2 minutes or until the desired doneness of eggs.
8. Remove from heat and immediately, place the cheese in the center of omelet.
9. Fold the edges of omelet over cheese and cut into 2 portions.
10. Serve immediately.

Nutritional Information per Serving
Calories: 633
Fat: 49.3g
Sat Fat: 20.7g
Cholesterol: 400mg
Sodium: 1500mg
Carbohydrates: 2g
Fiber: 0g

Sugar: 1g

Protein: 41.2g

Chicken & Asparagus Frittata

One of the best skillet breakfast meal that will satisfy you in a delish way...This frittata is super flavorful and healthy as well.

Yield: 4 servings

Preparation time: 15 minutes

Cooking time: 12 minutes

Allergens: egg, dairy

Ingredients:

- ½ cup grass-fed cooked chicken, chopped
- 1/3 cup Parmesan cheese, grated
- 6 organic eggs, beaten lightly
- Salt and ground black pepper, as required
- 1 teaspoon unsalted butter
- ½ cup boiled asparagus, chopped
- 1 tablespoon fresh parsley, chopped

Instructions:

1. Preheat the broiler of oven.
2. In a bowl, add the cheese, eggs, salt, and black pepper and beat until well combined.
3. In a large ovenproof skillet, melt butter over medium-high heat and cook the chicken and asparagus for about 2-3 minutes.
4. Add the egg mixture and stir to combine.
5. Cook for about 4-5 mins.
6. Remove from the heat and sprinkle with the parsley.
7. Now, transfer the skillet under broiler and broil for about 3-4 minutes or until slightly puffed.
8. Cut into desired sized wedges and serve immediately.

Nutritional Information per Serving

Calories: 157

Fat: 9.7g

Sat Fat: 3.6g

Cholesterol: 260mg

Sodium: 207mg

Carbohydrates: 1.2g

Fiber: 0.4g

Sugar: 0.8g

Protein: 16.5g

Mixed Veggies Quiche

Enjoy fresh garden veggies in this versatile and flavorsome breakfast recipe...This flavorsome quiche is loaded with the goodness of fresh garden veggies.

Yield: 4 servings

Preparation time: 20 minutes

Cooking time: 20 minutes

Allergens: egg, dairy, nuts

Ingredients:

- 6 organic eggs
- ½ cup unsweetened almond milk
- Salt and ground black pepper, as required
- 1 cup fresh baby spinach, chopped
- 1 cup fresh baby kale, chopped
- ½ cup green bell pepper, seeded and chopped
- 1 scallion, chopped
- ¼ cup fresh cilantro, chopped
- 1 tablespoon fresh chives, minced
- 3 tablespoons mozzarella cheese, grated

Instructions:

1. Preheat your oven to 400° F (200° c). Lightly grease a pie dish.
2. In a large bowl, add the eggs, almond milk, salt, and black pepper and beat until well combined.
3. Set aside.
4. In another bowl, add the vegetables and herbs and mix well.
5. In the bottom of the prepared pie dish, place the veggie mixture evenly and top with the egg mixture.
6. Bake for 20 minutes or until a wooden skewer inserted in the center comes out clean.
7. Remove from the oven and sprinkle with the Parmesan cheese.
8. Set aside for about 5 minutes before slicing.
9. Cut into desired sized wedges and serve warm.

Nutritional Information per Serving

Calories: 176

Fat: 10.9g

Sat Fat: 4.3g

Cholesterol: 257mg

Sodium: 296mg

Carbohydrates: 5g

Fiber: 0.9g

Sugar: 1.4g
Protein: 15.4g

Salad Recipes

Tomato, Basil & Mozzarella Salad

A lovely tomato salad with a refreshing herbed touch... This salad is perfect to enjoy summer flavors of fresh tomatoes and herbs.

Yield: 6 servings

Preparation time: 15 minutes

Allergens: dairy

Ingredients:

- 4 cups cherry tomatoes, halved
- 1½ pounds mozzarella cheese, cubed
- ¼ cup fresh basil leaves, chopped
- ¼ cup olive oil
- 2 tablespoons fresh lemon juice
- 1 teaspoon fresh oregano, minced
- 1 teaspoon fresh parsley, minced
- 2-4 drops liquid stevia
- Salt and ground black pepper, as required

Instructions:

1. In a salad bowl, mix together tomatoes, mozzarella, and basil.
2. In a small bowl, add remaining ingredients and beat until well combined.
3. Place dressing over salad and toss to coat well.
4. Serve immediately.

Nutritional Information per Serving

Calories: 116

Fat: 10g

Sat Fat: 2g

Cholesterol: 14mg

Sodium: 77mg

Carbohydrates: 5.2g

Fiber: 1.6g
Sugar: 3.3g
Protein: 3.2g

Cucumber & Spinach Salad

One of the best crunchy salads with the refreshing touch of dressing... This creamy dressing compliments the crunch of veggies nicely.

Yield: 6 servings

Preparation time: 15 minutes

Allergens: dairy

Ingredients:

For Dressing:

- 5 tablespoons olive oil
- 4 tablespoons plain Greek yogurt
- 2 tablespoons fresh lemon juice
- 2 tablespoons fresh mint leaves, chopped finely
- 1 teaspoon Erythritol
- Salt and ground black pepper, as required

For Salad:

- 3 cups cucumbers, peeled, seeded and sliced
- 10 cups fresh baby spinach
- ¼ of medium yellow onion, sliced

Instructions:

1. For dressing: Add all ingredients in a bowl and beat until well combined.
2. Cover and refrigerate to chill for about 1 hour.
3. In a large serving bowl, add all salad ingredients and mix.
4. Place dressing over salad and toss to coat well.
5. Serve immediately.

Nutritional Information per Serving

Calories: 130

Fat: 12.1g

Sat Fat: 1.9g

Cholesterol: 1mg

Sodium: 77mg

Carbohydrates: 5.1g

Fiber: 1.6g

Sugar: 2.1g

Protein: 2.5g

Cheesy Broccoli Salad

A lovely bowl of colors and flavors... The lemony dressing makes a perfect match with strawberries and broccoli.

Yield: 10 servings

Preparation time: 15 minutes

Allergens: dairy

Ingredients:

For Salad:

- 8 cups small fresh broccoli florets
- 1 (8-ounce) package Colby-Monterey Jack cheese, cubed
- 2 cups fresh strawberries, hulled and sliced
- ¼ cup fresh mint leaves, chopped

For Dressing:

- 1 cup mayonnaise
- 1 teaspoon balsamic vinegar
- 2 teaspoons Erythritol
- Salt and ground black pepper, as required

Instructions:

1. For the salad: in a large serving bowl, add all the ingredients and mix well.
2. For dressing: in another bowl, add all the ingredients and beat until well combined.
3. Pour the dressing over salad and gently, stir to combine.
4. Serve immediately.

Nutritional Information per Serving

Calories: 374

Fat: 35.2g

Sat Fat: 226g

Cholesterol: 105mg

Sodium: 184mg

Carbohydrates: 11g

Fiber: 4.8g

Sugar: 4.5g

Protein: 6.3g

Cabbage & Onion Salad

One of the best crunchy and creamy cabbage salad with the refreshing tanginess of lime juice… This salad will brighten up any barbecue party table.

Yield: 6 servings

Preparation time: 15 minutes

Allergens: dairy

Ingredients:

For Salad:

- 4 cups green cabbage, shredded
- ¼ onion, sliced thinly
- 1 teaspoon lime zest, grated freshly
- 3 tablespoons fresh cilantro, chopped

For Dressing:

- ¾ cup mayonnaise
- 2 teaspoons fresh lime juice
- 2 teaspoons chili sauce
- ½ teaspoon Erythritol
- 2 garlic cloves, minced

Instructions:

1. For the salad: in a large bowl, add all the ingredients and mix.
2. For dressing: in another bowl, add all the ingredients and beat until well combined.
3. Place dressing over salad and gently, toss to coat well.
4. Cover and refrigerate to chill before serving.

Nutritional Information per Serving

Calories: 196

Fat: 20.1g

Sat Fat: 3g

Cholesterol: 10mg

Sodium: 231mg

Carbohydrates: 3.6g

Fiber: 1.3g

Sugar: 1.7g

Protein: 0.7g

Mixed Veggie Salad

A phenomenal salad with the combination of fresh vegetables and creamy yogurt dressing... This salad will be great for a healthy lunch.

Yield: 6 servings

Preparation time: 20 minutes

Allergens: dairy

Ingredients:

For Dressing:

- 1 small avocado, peeled, pitted and chopped
- ¼ cup plain Greek yogurt
- 1 small yellow onion, chopped
- 1 garlic clove, chopped
- 2 tablespoons fresh parsley
- 2 tablespoons fresh lemon juice

For Salad:

- 6 cups fresh spinach, shredded
- 2 medium zucchinis, cut into thin slices
- ½ cup celery, sliced
- ½ cup red bell pepper, seeded and sliced thinly

- ½ cup yellow onion, sliced thinly
- ½ cup cucumber, sliced thinly
- ½ cup cherry tomatoes, halved
- ¼ cup Kalamata olives, pitted
- ½ cup feta cheese, crumbled

Instructions:

1. For dressing: in a food processor, add all the ingredients and pulse until smooth.
2. For the salad: in a salad bowl, add all the ingredients and mix well.
3. Pour the dressing over salad and gently, toss to coat well.
4. Serve immediately.

Nutritional Information per Serving
Calories: 148
Fat: 10.3g
Sat Fat: 3.5g
Cholesterol: 12mg
Sodium: 238mg
Carbohydrates: 11.1g
Fiber: 4.6g
Sugar: 4.4g
Protein: 5.3g

Creamy Lobster Salad

A great and tasty recipe of wonderfully creamy lobster salad... This creamy lobster salad will be a great hit for a crowd at lunchtime.

Yield: 14 servings

Preparation time: 15 minutes

Allergens: dairy

Ingredients:

- 5 pounds cooked lobster meat, shredded
- 3 yellow bell peppers, seeded and chopped
- 6 celery stalks, chopped
- 1 large yellow onion, chopped
- 2 cups mayonnaise
- Freshly ground black pepper, as required

Instructions:

1. In a bowl, add all ingredients and mix until well combined.
2. Refrigerate to chill before serving.

Nutritional Information per Serving

Calories: 364

Fat: 24.3g

Sat Fat: 3.8g

Cholesterol: 248mg

Sodium: 1000mg

Carbohydrates: 3.2g

Fiber: 0.7g

Sugar: 1.8g

Protein: 31.2g

Shrimp &Green Beans Salad

A simple recipe that makes a comforting and delicious salad... Broiled shrimp and green beans come together nicely to create an unforgettable salad.

Yield: 5 servings

Preparation time: 20 minutes

Cooking time: 8 minutes

Allergens: dairy

Ingredients:

For Shrimp:

- 2 tablespoons olive oil
- 2 tablespoons fresh key lime juice
- 4 large garlic cloves, peeled
- 2 sprigs fresh rosemary leaves
- ½ teaspoon garlic salt
- 20 large shrimp, peeled and deveined

For Salad:

- 1 pound fresh green beans, trimmed
- ¼ cup olive oil

- 1 onion, sliced
- Salt and ground black pepper, as required
- ½ cup garlic and herb feta cheese, crumbled

Instructions:

1. For shrimp marinade: in a blender, add all the ingredients except shrimp and pulse until smooth.
2. Transfer the marinade in a large bowl.
3. Add the shrimp and coat with marinade generously.
4. Cover the bowl and refrigerate to marinate for at least 30 minutes.
5. Preheat the broiler of oven. Arrange the rack in the top position of the oven. Line a large baking sheet with a piece of foil.
6. Place the shrimp with marinade onto the prepared baking sheet.
7. Broil for about 3-4 minutes per side.
8. Transfer the shrimp mixture into a bowl and refrigerate until using.
9. Meanwhile, for salad: in a pan of the salted boiling water, add the green beans and cook for about 3-4 minutes.
10. Drain the green beans well and rinse under cold running water.
11. Transfer the green beans into a large bowl.

12. Add the onion, shrimp, salt and black pepper and stir to combine.
13. Cover and refrigerate to chill for about 1 hour.
14. Stir in cheese just before serving.

Nutritional Information per Serving

Calories: 303

Fat: 18.5g

Sat Fat: 4.7g

Cholesterol: 100mg

Sodium: 420mg

Carbohydrates: 11g

Fiber: 4g

Sugar: 2.5g

Protein: 24.3g

Shrimp & Veggies Salad

An unforgettable and flavorsome salad of shrimp and fresh veggies...This delicious salad will be a great hit for summer entertaining.

Yield: 6 servings

Preparation time: 20 minutes

Cooking time: 5 minutes

Allergens: nuts

Ingredients:

For Dressing:

- 2 tablespoons natural almond butter
- 1 garlic clove, crushed
- 1 tablespoon fresh cilantro, chopped
- 2 tablespoons fresh lime juice
- 1 tablespoon yacon syrup
- ½ teaspoon cayenne pepper
- ¼ teaspoon salt
- 1 tablespoon water
- 1/3 cup olive oil

For Salad:

- 1 pound shrimp, peeled and deveined
- Salt and ground black pepper, as required
- 1 teaspoon olive oil
- 1 cup carrot, peeled and julienned
- 1 cup red cabbage, shredded
- 1 cup green cabbage, shredded
- 1 cup cucumber, julienned
- 4 cups fresh baby arugula
- ¼ cup fresh basil, chopped
- ¼ cup fresh cilantro, chopped
- 4 cups lettuce, torn
- ¼ cup almonds, chopped

Instructions:

1. For dressing: in a bowl, add all ingredients except oil and beat until well combined.
2. Slowly, add oil, beating continuously until smooth.
3. For the salad: in a bowl, add shrimp, salt, black pepper, and oil and toss to coat well.
4. Heat a skillet over medium heat and cook shrimp for about 2 minutes per side.
5. Remove from the heat and set aside to cool.

6. In a large serving bowl, add all the cooked shrimp, remaining salad ingredients and dressing and toss to coat well.
7. Serve immediately.

Nutritional Information per Serving
Calories: 270
Fat: 17.5g
Sat Fat: 2.6g
Cholesterol: 159mg
Sodium: 318mg
Carbohydrates: 10g
Fiber: 2.7g
Sugar: 4.5g
Protein: 20.2g

Salmon & Egg Salad

One of the healthiest versions in dinner salads... Try this salad recipe, which is even more nutritious than tuna salad for a nice change of pace...

Yield: 8 servings

Preparation time: 15 minutes

Allergens: egg, dairy

Ingredients:

- 12 hard-boiled organic eggs, peeled and cubed
- 1 pound cooked salmon, chopped
- 3 celery stalks, chopped
- 1 yellow onion, chopped
- 4 tablespoons fresh dill, chopped
- 2 cups mayonnaise
- Salt and ground black pepper, as required
- 8 cups fresh lettuce leaves

Instructions:

1. In a large serving bowl, add all the ingredients except the lettuce leaves and gently stir to combine.

2. Cover and refrigerate to chill before serving.
3. Divide the lettuce onto serving plates and top with the salmon salad.
4. Serve immediately.

Nutritional Information per Serving

Calories: 547

Fat: 50.3g

Sat Fat: 8.6g

Cholesterol: 291mg

Sodium: 509mg

Carbohydrates: 3.5g

Fiber: 1g

Sugar: 1.7g

Protein: 20.1g

Chicken, Spinach & Strawberry Salad

A wonderful bowl of chicken, fresh strawberries and fresh spinach... These grilled chicken breasts receive a double dose of deliciousness from strawberries and dressing.

Yield: 8 servings

Preparation time: 20 minutes

Cooking time: 16 minutes

Allergens: absent

Ingredients:

- 2 pounds grass-fed boneless, skinless chicken breasts
- ½ cup olive oil
- ¼ cup fresh lemon juice
- 2 tablespoons Erythritol
- 1 garlic clove, minced
- Salt and ground black pepper, as required
- 4 cups fresh strawberries
- 8 cups fresh spinach, torn

Instructions:

1. For marinade: in a large bowl, add oil, lemon juice, Erythritol, garlic, salt, and black pepper and beat until well combined.
2. In a large resealable plastic bag, place chicken and ¾ cup marinade.
3. Seal bag and shake to coat well.
4. Refrigerate overnight.
5. Cover the bowl of remaining marinade and refrigerate before serving.
6. Preheat the grill to medium heat. Grease the grill grate.
7. Remove the chicken from bag and discard the marinade.

8. Place the chicken onto grill grate and grill, covered for about 5-8 minutes per side.
9. Remove chicken from grill and cut into bite sized pieces.
10. In a large bowl, add the chicken pieces, strawberries and spinach, and mix.
11. Place the reserved marinade and toss to coat.
12. Serve immediately.

Nutritional Information per Serving
Calories: 356
Fat: 21.4g
Sat Fat: 4.g
Cholesterol: 101mg
Sodium: 143mg
Carbohydrates: 6.1g
Fiber: 2.1g
Sugar: 3.8g
Protein: 34.2g

Ground Turkey & Veggies Salad

A filling salad that will be a great addition to your holiday dinner recipes...This lovely salad is full of contrasting flavors of turkey and veggies.

Yield: 6 servings

Preparation time: 13 minutes

Cooking time: 20 minutes

Allergens: nuts

Ingredients:

- 1 pound ground turkey
- 1 tablespoon olive oil
- Salt and ground black pepper, as required
- ¼ cup water
- ½ of English cucumber, chopped
- 4 cups green cabbage, shredded
- ½ cup fresh mint leaves, chopped
- 2 tablespoons fresh lime juice
- ¼ cup walnuts, chopped

Instructions:

1. Heat oil in a large skillet over medium-high and cook the turkey for about 6-8 mins, breaking up the pieces with a spatula.
2. Stir in the water and cook for about 4-5 minutes or until almost all the liquid is evaporated.
3. Remove from the heat and transfer the turkey into a bowl.
4. Set the bowl aside to cool completely.
5. In a large serving bowl, add the vegetables, mint and lime juice and mix well.
6. Add the cooked turkey and stir to combine.
7. Serve immediately.

Nutritional Information per Serving

Calories: 219

Fat: 13.8g

Sat Fat: 1.9g

Cholesterol: 77mg

Sodium: 120mg

Carbohydrates: 4.8g

Fiber: 2.2g

Sugar: 2g

Protein: 22.9g

Ground Beef Salad

When you want a hearty salad that's different from the usual, this taco salad hits the spot... This filling dinner salad features authentic Mexican flavors.

Yield: 6 servings

Preparation time: 20 minutes

Cooking time: 10 minutes

Allergens: dairy

Ingredients:

- 1 pound grass-fed ground beef
- 1 teaspoon olive oil
- 1 tablespoon taco seasoning
- 8 ounces Romaine lettuce, chopped
- 1 1/3 cups grape tomatoes, halved
- 1 large cucumber, chopped
- ½cup scallions, chopped
- ¾cup Cheddar cheese, shredded
- 1/3 cup salsa
- 1/3 cup sour cream

Instructions:

8. In a skillet, heat oil over high heat and stir fry beef for about 8-10 minutes, breaking up the pieces with a spatula.
9. Stir in taco seasoning and remove from the heat.
10. Set aside to cool slightly.
11. Meanwhile, in a large bowl, add the remaining ingredients and mix until well combined.
12. Add the ground beef and toss to coat well.
13. Serve immediately.

Nutritional Information per Serving

Calories: 256

Fat: 15.7g

Sat Fat: 7.8g

Cholesterol: 71mg

Sodium: 343mg

Carbohydrates: 7.8g

Fiber: 1.4g

Sugar: 3.2g

Protein: 20.5g

Soup & Stew Recipes

Avocado & Bacon Soup

One of the quite comforting and creamy soups without the use of any dairy... Avocado is the key ingredient for the creaminess of this soup.

Yield: 6 servings

Preparation time: 10 minutes

Cooking time: 5 minutes

Allergens: absent

Ingredients:

- 4 cups homemade chicken broth
- 2 avocados, peeled, pitted and chopped
- 1/3 cup fresh cilantro, chopped roughly
- ½ teaspoon garlic, chopped roughly
- 1 teaspoon fresh lime juice
- ½ pound cooked bacon, chopped
- Salt and ground black pepper, as required

Instructions:

1. In a large pan, add the broth and bring to a boil.

2. Reduce the heat to low.
3. In a blender, add the avocadoes, cilantro, garlic and lime juice and pulse until chopped finely.
4. Add 1 cup of the chicken broth and pulse until smooth.
5. Transfer the avocado mixture into the pan of remaining simmering broth and stir to combine.
6. Stir in the bacon, salt, and pepper and remove from the heat.
7. Serve immediately.

Nutritional Information per Serving

Calories: 367

Fat: 29.8g

Sat Fat: 8.2g

Cholesterol: 42mg

Sodium: 1400mg

Carbohydrates: 7g

Fiber: 4.5g

Sugar: 0.8g

Protein: 18.5g

Bacon & Jalapeño Soup

A really delicious and comforting bowl of creamy and cheesy soup with hot spicy touch… Jalapeño peppers add a delicious heat in this soup.

Yield: 5 servings

Preparation time: 15 minutes

Cooking time: 22 minutes

Allergens: dairy

Ingredients:

- ¼ cup unsalted butter
- 4 medium jalapeño peppers, seeded and chopped
- 1 small yellow onion, chopped
- 1 teaspoon dried thyme, crushed
- ½ teaspoon ground cumin
- 3 cups homemade chicken broth
- 8 ounces cheddar cheese, shredded
- ¾ cup heavy cream
- Salt and ground black pepper, as required
- 6 cooked bacon slices, chopped

Instructions:

1. In a large pan, melt 1 tablespoon of the butter over medium heat and sauté the jalapeño peppers for about 1-2 minutes.
2. With a slotted spoon, transfer the jalapeño peppers onto a plate.
3. In the same pan, melt the remaining butter over medium heat and sauté the onion for about 3-4 minutes.
4. Add the spices and sauté for about 1 minute.
5. Add the broth and bring to a boil.
6. Reduce the heat to low and cook for about 10 minutes.
7. Remove from the heat and with an immersion blender, blend until smooth.
8. Return the pan over medium-low heat.
9. Stir in ¾ of the cooked bacon, cooked jalapeño, cheese, cream, and black pepper and cook for about 5 minutes.
10. Serve hot with the topping of remaining bacon.

Nutritional Information per Serving

Calories: 549

Fat: 46.5g

Sat Fat: 24.6g

Cholesterol: 135mg
Sodium: 1900mg
Carbohydrates: 4.5g
Fiber: 0.9g
Sugar: 1.7g
Protein: 27.9g

Broccoli Soup

One of the greatly flavored and delicious broccoli soup with richly cheesy touch... This soup will be a hit for family and friend's gatherings.

Yield: 5 servings

Preparation time: 10 minutes

Cooking time: 15 minutes

Allergens: dairy

Ingredients:

- 4 cups homemade chicken broth
- 20 ounces small broccoli florets
- 12 ounces cheddar cheese, cubed
- Salt and ground black pepper, as required
- 1 cup heavy cream

Instructions:

1. In a large soup pan, add the broth and broccoli over medium-high heat and bring to a boil.
2. Reduce the heat to low and cook, covered for about 5-7 minutes.
3. Stir in the cheese and cook for about 2-3 minutes, stirring continuously.
4. Stir in the salt, black pepper and cream and cook for about 2 minutes.
5. Serve hot.

Nutritional Information per Serving

Calories: 426

Fat: 32.9g

Sat Fat: 20.2g

Cholesterol: 104mg

Sodium: 1000mg

Carbohydrates: 9g

Fiber: 3g
Sugar: 2.9g
Protein: 24.5g

Yellow Squash Soup

One of the delicious and nourishing yellow squash soup...
yellow squash, Parmesan cheese, and lemon juice combine
with each other nicely.

Yield: 6 servings

Preparation time: 15 minutes

Cooking time: 35 minutes

Allergens: dairy

Ingredients:

- 2 tablespoons unsalted butter
- 2 yellow onions, chopped
- 6 garlic cloves, minced
- 6 cups yellow squash, seeded and cubed
- 4 thyme sprigs
- 4 cups homemade vegetable broth
- Salt and ground black pepper, as required
- 2 tablespoons fresh lemon juice
- 4 tablespoons Parmesan cheese, shredded
- 2 teaspoons fresh lemon peel, grated finely

Instructions:

1. In a large soup pan, melt butter over medium heat and sauté the onions for about 5-6 minutes.
2. Add garlic and sauté for about 1 minute.
3. Add the yellow squash cubes and cook for about 5 minutes.
4. Stir in the thyme, broth, salt, and black pepper and bring to a boil.
5. Reduce the heat to low and cook, covered for about 15-20 minutes.
6. Remove from the heat and discard the thyme sprigs.
7. Set the pan aside to cool slightly.
8. In a large blender, add the soup in batches and process until smooth.
9. Return the soup into the same pan over medium heat.
10. Stir in the lemon juice and cook for about 2-3 minutes or until heated completely.
11. Serve hot with the garnishing of cheese and lemon peel.

Nutritional Information per Serving
Calories: 115
Fat: 6g

Sat Fat: 3.4g

Cholesterol: 13mg

Sodium: 634mg

Carbohydrates: 9.8g

Fiber: 2.5g

Sugar: 4.2g

Protein: 6.6g

Chicken Soup

One of the comforting and nourishing soups for dinner...
Chicken and veggies make a really delicious bowl of soup.

Yield: 4 servings

Preparation time: 15 minutes

Cooking time: 25 minutes

Allergens: dairy

Ingredients:

- 2 tablespoons butter
- 1 medium carrot, peeled and chopped
- ½ cup yellow onion, chopped
- 2 celery stalks, chopped
- 1 garlic clove, minced
- 2 teaspoons xanthan gum
- 1 teaspoon dried parsley, crushed
- Salt and ground black pepper, as required
- 4 cups homemade chicken broth
- 10 ounces cauliflower, chopped
- 2 cups cooked grass-fed chicken, chopped
- 2 cups heavy cream

- ¼ cup fresh parsley, chopped

Instructions:

1. In a large soup pan, melt butter over medium heat and sauté the carrot, onion, and celery for about 3-4 minutes.
2. Add garlic and sauté for about 1 minute.
3. Meanwhile, in a bowl, mix together the xanthan gum, parsley, salt, and black pepper.
4. Stir in the parsley mixture, broth and cauliflower and bring to a boil.
5. Reduce the heat to low and cook, covered for about 15 minutes, stirring occasionally.
6. Stir in cooked chicken, cream, parsley and salt and cook for about 4-5 minutes.
7. Serve hot.

Nutritional Information per Serving
Calories: 442
Fat: 31.6g
Sat Fat: 18.5g
Cholesterol: 151mg
Sodium: 986mg
Carbohydrates: 11g
Fiber: 4.4g

Sugar: 4g
Protein: 28.4g

Meatballs Soup

A restaurant-style homemade soup... This hearty soup is a combo of tender meatballs and kale with a flavorful broth.

Yield: 6 servings

Preparation time: 20 minutes

Cooking time: 25 minutes

Allergens: egg, dairy

Ingredients:

For Meatballs:

- 1 pound lean ground turkey
- 1 garlic clove, minced
- 1 organic egg, beaten
- ¼ cup Parmesan cheese, grated
- Salt and ground black pepper, as required

For Soup:

- 1 tablespoon olive oil
- 1 small yellow onion, chopped finely
- 1 garlic clove, minced
- 6 cups homemade chicken broth
- 8 cups fresh kale, trimmed and chopped
- 2 organic eggs, beaten lightly
- Salt and ground black pepper, as required

Instructions:

1. For meatballs: in a bowl, add all ingredients and mix until well combined.
2. Make equal sized small balls from the mixture.
3. In a large soup pan, heat oil over medium heat and sauté onion for about 5-6 minutes.
4. Add garlic and sauté for about 1 minute.
5. Add the broth and bring to a boil.
6. Carefully, place the balls in the pan and bring to a boil.

7. Reduce heat to low and simmer for about 10 minutes.
8. Stir in kale and bring the soup to a gentle simmer.
9. Simmer for about 2-3 minutes.
10. Slowly, add the beaten eggs, stirring continuously.
11. Season with the salt and black pepper and serve hot.

Nutritional Information per Serving

Calories:288

Fat: 14g

Sat Fat: 4.8g

Cholesterol: 146mg

Sodium: 1171mg

Carbohydrates: 12g

Fiber: 1.6g

Sugar: 1.4g

Protein: 29.3g

Beef Stew

One of the delicious stew with a touch of exoticness... This stew is filled with the delish flavors of beef, cabbage, and tomatoes.

Yield: 8 servings

Preparation time: 15 minutes

Cooking time: 1 hour 50 minutes

Allergens: absent

Ingredients:

- 2 pounds grass-fed beef stew meat, trimmed and cubed into 1-inch size
- 1 1/3 cups homemade hot chicken broth
- 2 yellow onions, chopped
- 2 bay leaves
- 1 teaspoon Greek seasoning
- Salt and ground black pepper, as required
- 3 celery stalks, chopped
- 1 (8-ounce) package shredded cabbage
- 1 (6-ounce) can sugar-free tomato sauce

- 1 (8-ounce) can sugar-free whole plum tomatoes, chopped roughly with liquid

Instructions:

1. Heat a large nonstick pan over medium-high heat and cook the beef for about 4-5 minutes or until browned.
2. Drain excess grease from the pan.
3. Stir in the broth, onion, bay leaves, Greek seasoning, salt, and black pepper and bring it to a boil.
4. Reduce heat to low and cook covered for about 1¼ hours.
5. Stir in the celery and cabbage and cook, covered for about 30 minutes.
6. Stir in the tomato sauce and chopped plum tomatoes and cook, uncovered for about 15-20 minutes.
7. Stir in the salt and remove from heat.
8. Discard bay leaves and serve hot.

Nutritional Information per Serving

Calories: 247

Fat: 7.5g

Sat Fat: 2.8g

Cholesterol: 101mg

Sodium: 346mg

Carbohydrates: 7g

Fiber: 2.1g

Sugar: 3.9g

Protein: 36.5g

Lamb Stew

A wonderfully delicious stew that will warm you up very nicely in a chilly night... Surely you would love to enjoy this stew.

Yield: 8 servings

Preparation time: 15 minutes

Cooking time: 2¼ hours

Allergens: absent

Ingredients:

- 1 teaspoon ground coriander
- ¾ teaspoon ground cumin
- ½ teaspoon cayenne pepper
- 2 tablespoons coconut oil
- 3 pounds grass-fed lamb stew meat, cubed
- Salt and ground black pepper, as required
- ½ yellow onion, chopped
- 2 garlic cloves, minced
- 2 cups homemade chicken broth
- 1 (15-ounce) can sugar-free diced tomatoes
- 1 medium head cauliflower, cut into 1-inch florets

Instructions:

1. Preheat your oven to 300° F (150° C).
2. In a small bowl, mix together spices. Set aside.
3. In a large ovenproof pan, heat oil over medium heat and cook lamb with salt and black pepper for about 10 minutes or until browned from all sides.
4. Transfer the lamb into a bowl.
5. In the same pan, add onion and sauté for about 3-4 minutes.
6. Add the garlic and spice mixture and sauté for about 1 minute.
7. Add the cooked lamb, broth and tomatoes and bring to a gentle boil.
8. Immediately, cover the pan and transfer into the oven.
9. Bake for about 1½ hours.
10. Remove from the oven and stir in the cauliflower.
11. Bake covered for about 30 minutes more or until cauliflower is done completely.
12. Serve hot.

Nutritional Information per Serving

Calories: 379

Fat: 16.4g

Sat Fat: 7.5g

Cholesterol: 153mg

Sodium: 353mg

Carbohydrates: 5.2g

Fiber: 1.8g

Sugar: 2.7g

Protein: 50.3g

Catfish & Okra Stew

A sensational stew consisting of catfish and veggie mixture... Red pepper flakes and hot sauce add a delicious spicy touch in this hearty and filling stew.

Yield: 10 servings

Preparation time: 15 minutes

Cooking time: 50 minutes

Allergens: dairy

Ingredients:

- ¼ cup butter
- ½ cup yellow onion, chopped
- 1 cup celery stalk, chopped
- ½ cup green bell pepper, seeded and chopped
- 1 garlic clove, minced
- 4 cups water
- 4 beef bouillon cubes
- 20 ounces okra, trimmed and chopped
- 2 (14-ounce) cans sugar-free diced tomatoes with liquid
- 2 bay leaves

- 1 teaspoon dried thyme, crushed
- 2 teaspoons red pepper flakes, crushed
- ¼ teaspoon hot pepper sauce
- Salt and ground black pepper, as required
- 32 ounces catfish fillets
- ½ cup fresh cilantro, chopped
- 1 cup sour cream

Instructions:

1. In a large skillet, melt butter over medium heat and sauté the onion, celery and bell pepper for about 4-5 minutes.
2. Meanwhile, in a large soup pan, mix together bouillon cubes and water and bring to a boil over medium heat.
3. Transfer the onion mixture and remaining ingredients except for catfish into the pan of boiling water and bring it to a boil.
4. Reduce the heat to low and cook, covered for about 30 minutes.
5. Stir in catfish fillets and cook for about 10-15 minutes.
6. Stir in the cilantro and remove from the heat.
7. Serve hot with the topping of the sour cream.

Nutritional Information per Serving

Calories: 261

Fat: 16.8g

Sat Fat: 7.3g

Cholesterol: 65mg

Sodium: 373mg

Carbohydrates: 10.3g

Fiber: 3.3g

Sugar: 3.9g

Protein: 17.2g

Seafood Stew

One of the comforting and nourishing soup... The combo of fish, seafood, basil, and lime makes a delicious bowl of soup.

Yield: 6 servings

Preparation time: 20 minutes

Cooking time: 30 minutes

Allergens: butter, mayonnaise

Ingredients:

- 2 tablespoons butter
- 1 medium yellow onion, chopped
- 2 garlic cloves, minced
- 1 Serrano pepper, chopped
- ¼ teaspoon red pepper flakes, crushed
- ¾ pound fresh tomatoes, chopped
- 1½ cups fish broth
- 1 pound red snapper fillets, cubed
- ½ pound shrimp, peeled and deveined
- ¼ pound fresh squid, cleaned and cut into rings
- ¼ pound bay scallops

- ¼ pound mussels
- 2 tablespoons fresh lime juice
- ½ cup fresh basil, chopped
- 1/3 cup mayonnaise

Instructions:

1. In a large soup pan, melt butter over medium heat and sauté the onion for about 5-6 minutes.
2. Add the garlic, Serrano pepper, and red pepper flakes and sauté for about 1 minute.
3. Add tomatoes and broth and bring to a gentle simmer.
4. Reduce the heat and cook for about 10 minutes.
5. Add the tilapia and cook for about 2 minutes.
6. Stir in the remaining seafood and cook for about 6-8 minutes.
7. Stir in the lemon juice, basil, salt, and black pepper and remove from heat.
8. Serve hot.

Nutritional Information per Serving
Calories: 307
Fat: 11.6g
Sat Fat: 3.9g

Cholesterol: 185mg

Sodium: 443mg

Carbohydrates: 9g

Fiber: 1.2g

Sugar: 3.2g

Protein: 39.2g

Veggie Stew

A delicious vegetarian stew with a delish spicy touch...
Warm spices infuse this delicious veggie stew very nicely.

Yield: 4 servings

Preparation time: 20 minutes

Cooking time: 35 minutes

Allergens: absent

Ingredients:

- 2 tablespoons olive oil
- 1 yellow onion, chopped
- 2 teaspoons fresh ginger, grated
- 1 teaspoon ground turmeric
- 1 teaspoon ground cumin
- Salt and ground black pepper, as required
- 1-2 cups water, divided
- 1 cup cabbage, shredded
- 1 cup broccoli, chopped
- 2 large carrots, peeled and sliced

Instructions:

1. In a large soup pan, heat the oil over medium heat and sauté onion for about 5 minutes.
2. Stir in the ginger and spices and sauté for about 1 minute.
3. Add 1 cup of water and bring to a boil.
4. Reduce heat to medium-low and cook for about 10 minutes.
5. Add the vegetables and enough water that covers the half of vegetable mixture and stir to combine.
6. Increase the heat to medium-high and bring to a boil.
7. Reduce the heat to medium-low and cook, covered for about 10-15 minutes, stirring occasionally.
8. Serve hot.

Nutritional Information per Serving

Calories: 105

Fat: 7.4g

Sat Fat: 1.1g

Cholesterol: 0mg

Sodium: 77mg

Carbohydrates: 9g

Fiber: 2.8g

Sugar: 4g

Protein: 1.7g

Poultry Recipes

Butter Chicken

One of the best recipe to prepare a butter chicken at home... Surely this homemade butter chicken will fill your home with a fantastic aroma.

Yield: 5 servings

Preparation time: 15 minutes

Cooking time: 25 minutes

Allergens: dairy

Ingredients:

- 2 tablespoons unsalted butter
- 1 medium yellow onion, chopped
- 2 garlic cloves, minced
- 1 teaspoon fresh ginger, minced
- 1½ pounds grass-fed chicken breasts, cut into ¾-inch chunks
- 1 (6-ounce) can sugar-free tomato paste
- 1 tablespoon garam masala
- 1 teaspoon red chili powder
- 1 teaspoon ground cumin
- Salt and ground black pepper, as required
- 1 cup heavy cream
- 2 tablespoons fresh cilantro, chopped

Instructions:

1. In a large skillet, melt butter over medium-high heat and sauté the onions for about 4-5 minutes.
2. Add the garlic and ginger and sauté for about 1 minute.
3. Add the chicken, tomato paste and spices and cook for about 6-8 minutes or until the desired doneness of chicken.
4. Stir in heavy cream and cook for about 8-10 minutes, stirring occasionally.
5. Serve hot with the garnishing of cilantro.

Nutritional Information per Serving

Calories: 425

Fat: 24g

Sat Fat: 11.3g

Cholesterol: 166mg

Sodium: 233mg

Carbohydrates: 10.3g

Fiber: 2.2g

Sugar: 5.2g

Protein: 41.9g

Chicken & Veggie Curry

A super tasty curry with the heartiness of chicken, green beans and asparagus... Veggies and coconut milk compliment chicken greatly.

Yield: 4 servings

Preparation time: 15 minutes

Cooking time: 30 minutes

Allergens: absent

Ingredients:

- 1 pound grass-fed skinless, boneless chicken breasts, cubed
- 1 tablespoon olive oil
- 2 tablespoons green curry paste
- 1 cup unsweetened coconut milk
- 1 cup homemade chicken broth
- 1 cup asparagus spears, trimmed
- 1 cup green beans, trimmed
- Salt and ground black pepper, as required
- ¼ cup fresh cilantro leaves, chopped

Instructions:

1. In a skillet, heat oil over medium and sauté the curry paste for about 1-2 minutes.
2. Add the chicken and cook for about 8-10 minutes.
3. Add coconut milk and broth and bring to a boil.
4. Reduce the heat low and cook for about 8-10 minutes.
5. Add asparagus, green beans, salt, and black pepper and cook for about 4-5 minutes or until desired doneness.
6. Serve hot.

Nutritional Information per Serving

Calories: 385

Fat: 26.7g

Sat Fat: 14.8g

Cholesterol: 66mg

Sodium: 282mg

Carbohydrates: 9g

Fiber: 3g

Sugar: 3.2g

Protein: 29.5g

Chicken & Spinach in Creamy Sauce

A succulent chicken recipe that will become a favorite meal of the whole family... This classic recipe is packed with the flavors of chicken, spinach, cheese, and cream.

Yield: 4 servings

Preparation time: 15 minutes

Cooking time: 15 minutes

Allergens: dairy

Ingredients:

- 2 tablespoons butter, divided
- 1 pound grass-fed chicken tenders
- Salt and ground black pepper, as required
- 2 garlic cloves, minced
- 1 jalapeño pepper, chopped
- 10 ounces frozen spinach, thawed
- ¼ cup Parmesan cheese, shredded
- ¼ cup heavy cream

Instructions:

1. In a large skillet, melt 1 tablespoon of butter over medium-high heat and cook the chicken with salt and black pepper for about 2-3 minutes per side.
2. Transfer the chicken into a bowl.
3. In the same skillet, melt remaining butter over medium-low heat and sauté the garlic for about 1 minute.
4. Add the spinach and cook for about 1 minute.
5. Add the cheese, cream, salt, and black pepper and stir to combine.
6. Spread the spinach mixture in the bottom of skillet evenly.
7. Place chicken carefully over spinach in a single layer.
8. Immediately, reduce the heat to low and cook, covered for about 5 minutes.
9. Serve hot.

Nutritional Information per Serving
Calories: 333
Fat: 18.6g
Sat Fat: 8.6g
Cholesterol: 130mg
Sodium: 321mg
Carbohydrates: 3.7g
Fiber: 1.7g

Sugar: 0.5g
Protein: 37.1g

Bacon Wrapped Stuffed Chicken Breasts

A delicious way to use our garden fresh basil and tomatoes with chicken... This fabulous stuffing of basil, tomato, bacon, and cheese brightens the taste of chicken breasts.

Yield: 4 servings

Preparation time: 15 minutes

Cooking time: 33 minutes

Allergens: absent

Ingredients:

For Chicken Marinade:

- 3 tablespoons vinegar
- 3 tablespoons olive oil
- 2 tablespoons water
- 1 garlic clove, minced
- 1 teaspoon dried Italian seasoning
- ½ teaspoon dried rosemary
- Salt and ground black pepper, as required
- 4 (6-ounce) grass-fed skinless, boneless chicken breasts

For Stuffing:

- 16 fresh basil leaves
- 1 large fresh tomato, sliced thinly
- 4 provolone cheese slices
- 12 bacon slices
- ¼ cup Parmesan cheese, grated freshly

Instructions:

1. For marinade: In a bowl, add all ingredients except chicken and mix until well combined.
2. Place 1 chicken breasts onto a smooth surface.

3. Hold a sharp knife parallel to work surface, slice the chicken breast horizontally, without cutting all the way through.
4. Repeat with the remaining chicken breasts.
5. Place the breasts in the bowl of marinade and toss to coat well.
6. Refrigerate, covered for at least 30 minutes.
7. Preheat your oven to 500° F (260° C). Grease a baking dish.
8. Remove chicken breast from the bowl and arrange onto a smooth surface.
9. Place 4 basil leaves onto the bottom half of a chicken breast, followed by 2-3 tomato slices and 1 provolone cheese slice.
10. Now, fold the top half over filling.
11. Wrap the breast with 3 bacon slices and secure wit toothpicks.
12. Repeat with the remaining chicken breasts and filling.
13. Arrange breasts into the prepared baking dish in a single layer.
14. Bake for about 30 minutes, flipping one in the halfway through.
15. Remove from the oven and sprinkle each chicken breast with parmesan cheese evenly.
16. Bake for about 2-3 minutes more.
17. Serve hot.

Nutritional Information per Serving

Calories: 906

Fat: 62g

Sat Fat: 21.2g

Cholesterol: 219mg

Sodium: 240mg

Carbohydrates: 4.2g

Fiber: 0.7g

Sugar: 1.5g

Protein: 79.9g

Creamy Chicken Bake

A succulent chicken recipe that will become a favorite meal... The cream sauce with a touch of lemon and herbs gives the chicken a wonderful flavor.

Yield: 4 servings

Preparation time: 15 minutes

Cooking time: 1 hour 10 minutes

Allergens: dairy

Ingredients:

- 5 tablespoons unsalted butter, divided
- 2 small onions, sliced thinly
- 3 garlic cloves, minced
- 1 teaspoon dried tarragon, crushed
- 8 ounces cream cheese, softened
- 1 cup homemade chicken broth, divided
- 2 tablespoons fresh lemon juice
- ½ cup heavy cream
- 1½ teaspoons Herbs de Provence
- Salt and ground black pepper, as required
- 4 (6-ounce) grass-fed chicken breasts

Instructions:

1. Preheat your oven to 350° F (180° C). Grease a 13x9-inch baking dish with 1 tablespoon of butter.
2. In a skillet, melt 2 tablespoons of butter over medium heat and sauté the onion, garlic, and tarragon for about 4-5 minutes.
3. Transfer the onion mixture onto a plate.
4. In the same skillet, melt remaining 2 tablespoons of butter over low heat and cook the cream cheese, ½ cup of broth and lemon juice for about 3-4 minutes, stirring continuously.
5. Stir in the cream, Herbs de Provence, salt and black pepper and remove from heat.
6. Pour remaining broth in prepared baking dish.
7. Arrange chicken breasts in the baking dish in a single layer and top with the cream mixture evenly.
8. Bake for about 45-60 minutes.
9. Serve hot.

Nutritional Information per Serving
Calories: 729
Fat: 52.8g
Sat Fat: 28.7g
Cholesterol: 272mg

Sodium: 655mg
Carbohydrates: 6.4g
Fiber: 0.8g
Sugar: 2g
Protein: 55.8g

Chicken, Bacon& Broccoli Casserole

A satisfying dish that is delicious too... This one-pan creamy and cheesy chicken and broccoli dish is perfect for a busy weeknight.

Yield: 6 servings

Preparation time: 15 minutes

Cooking time: 35 minutes

Allergens: dairy

Ingredients:

For Chicken Mixture:

- 2 tablespoons butter
- ¼ cup cooked bacon, crumbled
- ½cup cheddar cheese, shredded
- 4 ounces cream cheese, softened
- ¼cup heavy whipping cream
- ½pack ranch seasoning mix
- 2/3 cup homemade chicken broth
- 1½ cups broccoli florets
- 2 cups cooked grass-fed chicken, shredded

For Topping:

- 2 cups cheddar cheese, shredded
- ½ cup cooked bacon, crumbled

Instructions:

1. Preheat your oven to 350° F (180° C). Arrange a rack in the upper portion of the oven.
2. For chicken mixture: in a large ovenproof skillet, melt butter over low heat.
3. Add the bacon, cheddar cheese, cream cheese, heavy whipping cream, ranch seasoning, and broth and with a wire whisk, beat until well combined.
4. Cook for about 5 minutes, stirring frequently.
5. Meanwhile, in a microwave-safe dish, place the broccoli and microwave until desired tenderness is achieved.
6. In the skillet, add the chicken and broccoli and mix until well combined.
7. Remove from the heat and top with the cheddar cheese, followed by the bacon.
8. Bake for about 25 minutes.
9. Now, set the oven to broiler.
10. Broil the chicken mixture for about 2-3 minutes or until cheese is bubbly.
11. Serve hot.

Nutritional Information per Serving

Calories: 666

Fat: 50.4g

Sat Fat: 25g

Cholesterol: 178mg

Sodium: 2008mg

Carbohydrates: 3.6g

Fiber: 0.6g

Sugar: 0.8g

Protein: 46.5g

3 Layers Chicken Casserole

A delectably flavorful casserole for dinner... Surely this rich and flavorful chicken casserole will be a great choice for a dinner party.

Yield: 6 servings

Preparation time: 15 minutes

Cooking time: 1 hour 10 minutes

Allergens: dairy

Ingredients:

For Chicken Layer:

- 6 (5-ounce) grass-fed skinless, boneless chicken breast
- Salt and ground black pepper, as required

For Bacon Layer:

- 5 bacon slices
- ¼ cup yellow onion, chopped
- ¼ cup jalapeño pepper, sliced
- ½ cup mayonnaise
- 1 (8-ounce) package cream cheese, softened

- ½ cup Parmesan cheese, shredded
- 1 cup cheddar cheese, shredded

For Topping:

- 1 package pork skins, crushed
- ¼ cup butter, melted
- ½ cup Parmesan cheese, shredded

Instructions:

1. Preheat your oven to 425° F (220° C). Grease a 13x9-inch casserole dish.
2. Arrange chicken breasts in a single layer and sprinkle with salt and black pepper.
3. Bake for about 30-40 minutes.
4. Meanwhile, for bacon layer: heat a nonstick skillet over medium heat.
5. Add the bacon and cook for about 8-10 minutes or until crispy.
6. With a slotted spoon, transfer the bacon onto a plate, leaving the grease into the skillet.
7. In the same skillet, add onion and sauté for about 4-5 minutes.
8. Remove from the heat and immediately, stir in bacon and remaining ingredients.

9. Remove casserole dish from oven and place bacon mixture over chicken breasts evenly.
10. In a bowl, mix together all topping ingredients.
11. Place the topping mixture over bacon mixture.
12. Now, reduce the oven temperature to 350° F.
13. Bake for about 15 minutes or until top becomes golden brown.
14. Serve hot.

Nutritional Information per Serving
Calories: 690
Fat: 48.9g
Sat Fat: 24.7g
Cholesterol: 197mg
Sodium: 1000mg
Carbohydrates: 7.1g
Fiber: 0.2g
Sugar: 1.8g
Protein: 55.2g

Spicy Roasted Turkey

A roasted turkey recipe that is simple to make... This roasted turkey will be a great hit for special holiday dinners.

Yield: 12 servings

Preparation time: 10 minutes

Cooking time: 3 hours 30 minutes

Allergens: dairy

Ingredients:

For Marinade:

- 1 (2-inch) piece fresh ginger, grated finely
- 3 large garlic cloves, crushed
- 1 green chili, chopped finely
- 1 teaspoon fresh lemon zest, grated finely
- 5 ounces plain Greek yogurt
- 3 tablespoons homemade tomato puree
- 2 tablespoons fresh lemon juice
- 1½ tablespoons garam masala
- 1 tablespoon ground cumin
- 2 teaspoons ground turmeric

For Turkey:

- 1 (9-pound) whole turkey, giblets, and neck removed
- Salt and ground black pepper, as required
- 1 garlic cloves, halved
- 1 lime, halved
- 1 lemon, halved

Instructions:

1. In a bowl, mix together all marinade ingredients.
2. With a fork, pierce the turkey completely.

3. In a large baking dish, place the turkey and rub with the marinade mixture evenly.
4. Refrigerate to marinate overnight.
5. Remove from refrigerator and set aside for about 30 minutes before cooking.
6. Preheat your oven to 390°F (198° C).
7. Sprinkle turkey with salt and black pepper evenly and stuff the cavity with garlic, lime, and lemon.
8. Arrange the turkey in a large roasting pan and roast for about 30 minutes.
9. Now, reduce the oven temperature to 350° F (180° C).
10. Roast for about 3 hours. (If skin becomes brown during roasting, then cover with a piece of foil).
11. Remove from the oven and palace the turkey onto a platter for about 15-20 minutes before carving.
12. With a sharp knife, cut the turkey into desired sized pieces and serve.

Nutritional Information per Serving

Calories: 595
Fat: 17.3g
Sat Fat: 5.8g
Cholesterol: 258mg
Sodium: 262mg
Carbohydrates: 2.3g
Fiber: 0.3g

Sugar: 1.2g
Protein: 100.3g

Spicy Ground Turkey

A delicious blend of turkey and tomatoes with aromatic spices... This spice mixture enhances the flavor of turkey greatly.

Yield: 4 servings

Preparation time: 15 minutes

Cooking time: 20 minutes

Allergens: dairy

Ingredients:

For Spices Blend:

- 1 teaspoon xanthan gum
- 1 teaspoon ground cumin
- 1 teaspoon ground coriander
- 1/8 teaspoon ground cloves
- 1/8 teaspoon ground cinnamon
- 1/8 teaspoon ground turmeric
- 1/8 teaspoon cayenne pepper
- 1 teaspoon salt
- 1/8 teaspoon freshly ground black pepper

For Turkey:

- 1¼ pounds ground turkey
- 1 small yellow onion, sliced
- 1 teaspoon fresh ginger, minced
- 1 teaspoon garlic, minced
- 1 medium tomato, chopped
- ½ cup water
- ½ cup unsweetened coconut milk
- 2 tablespoons fresh cilantro, chopped
- 2 tablespoons sour cream

Instructions:

1. For spice blend: Add all ingredients in a bowl and mix well.
2. Set aside.
3. Heat a nonstick skillet over medium-high heat and cook the turkey, onion, ginger, and garlic for about 5-6 minutes or until browned completely.
4. With a slotted spoon, discard any excess fat from the skillet.
5. Stir in the spice blend and cook for about 2 minutes, stirring frequently.
6. Stir in the remaining ingredients except for cilantro and bring to a gentle boil.
7. Reduce the heat to medium-low and simmer for about 10 minutes.

8. Stir in the cilantro and remove from the heat.

9. Serve immediately with the topping of sour cream.

Nutritional Information per Serving

Calories: 380

Fat: 24.2g

Sat Fat: 9.7g

Cholesterol: 147mg

Sodium: 763mg

Carbohydrates: 6.6g

Fiber: 2.5g

Sugar: 2.6g

Protein: 40.3g

Creamy Roasted Turkey Breast

One of the best way to prepare the turkey for family gatherings... The Italian dressing with seasoning adds moistness and delicious zip in turkey breast.

Yield: 14 servings

Preparation time: 15 minutes

Cooking time: 2½ hours

Allergens: dairy

Ingredients:

- 1 teaspoon onion powder
- ½ teaspoon garlic powder
- Salt and ground black pepper, as required
- 1 (7-pound) bone-in turkey breast
- 1½ cups Italian dressing

Instructions:

1. Preheat your oven to 325° F (170° C). Grease a 13x9-inch baking dish.

2. In a bowl, add onion powder, garlic powder, salt, and black pepper and mix well.

3. Rub the turkey breast with the seasoning mixture generously.

4. Arrange the turkey breast into the prepared baking dish and top with the Italian dressing evenly.

5. Bake for about 2-2½ hours, coating with pan juices occasionally.

6. Remove from the oven and palace the turkey breast onto a platter for about 10-15 minutes before slicing.

7. With a sharp knife, cut the turkey breast into desired sized slices and serve.

Nutritional Information per Serving

Calories: 459

Fat: 23.3g

Sat Fat: 5.2g

Cholesterol: 159mg

Sodium: 303mg

Carbohydrates: 2.8g

Fiber: 0g

Sugar: 2.2g

Protein: 48.7g

Turkey & Veggie Casserole

A delicious medley of turkey in tomato sauce and tender vegetables... This casserole will be a hit addition in your menu list.

Yield: 6 servings

Preparation time: 15 minutes

Cooking time: 50 minutes

Allergens: egg, dairy

Ingredients:

- 2 medium zucchinis, sliced
- 2 medium tomatoes, sliced
- ¾ pound ground turkey
- 1 large yellow onion, chopped
- 2 garlic cloves, minced
- 1 cup sugar-free tomato sauce
- ½ cup cheddar cheese, shredded
- 2 cups cottage cheese, shredded
- 1 organic egg yolk
- 1 tablespoon fresh rosemary, minced
- Salt and ground black pepper, as required

Instructions:

1. Preheat your oven to 500° F (260° C). Grease a large roasting pan
2. Arrange zucchini and tomato slices into the prepared roasting pan and spray with some cooking spray.
3. Roast for about 10-12 minutes.
4. Remove from oven and set aside.
5. Now, preheat your oven to 350° F (180° C).
6. Meanwhile, heat a nonstick skillet over medium-high heat and cook the turkey for about 4-5 minutes or until browned.
7. Add onion and garlic and sauté for about 4-5 minutes.
8. Stir in tomato sauce and cook for about 2-3 minutes.
9. Remove from the heat and place the turkey mixture into a 13x9-inch shallow baking dish.
10. In a bowl, add the remaining ingredients and mix until well combined.
11. Place the roasted vegetables over turkey mixture, followed by the cheese mixture evenly.
12. Bake for about 35 mins.
13. Remove from the oven and set aside for about 5-10 minutes.
14. Cut into equal sized 8 wedges and serve.

Nutritional Information per Serving

Calories: 266

Fat: 11.9g

Sat Fat: 4.3g

Cholesterol: 109mg

Sodium: 677mg

Carbohydrates: 11g

Fiber: 2.6g

Sugar: 5.3g

Protein: 30.7g

BBQ Turkey Pinwheel

An absolute delicious recipe of savory pinwheel... A blend of turkey, spinach, cheese, and spices make a surprisingly delicious pinwheel.

Yield: 8 servings

Preparation time: 15 minutes

Cooking time: 40 minutes

Allergens: egg, dairy

Ingredients:

For Meatloaf:

- 2 pounds ground turkey
- 1 cup cheddar cheese, shredded
- 1 tablespoon dried onion, minced
- 1 teaspoon dried garlic, minced
- 1 teaspoon garlic powder
- 1 teaspoon red chili powder
- 1 teaspoon ground mustard
- Salt, to taste
- 1 organic egg
- 2 ounces sugar-free BBQ sauce

For Topping:

- 2 ounces sugar-free BBQ sauce
- 5 cooked bacon slices, chopped
- ½ cup cheddar cheese, shredded

Instructions:

1. Preheat your oven to 400° F (200° C). Greased a 9x13-inch casserole dish.
2. For meatloaf: Add all ingredients in a bowl and mix until well combined.
3. Place the mixture into the prepared casserole dish evenly and press to smooth the surface.
4. Coat the top of meatloaf with BBQ sauce evenly and sprinkle with bacon, followed by the cheese.
5. Bake for approximately 40 minutes.
6. Remove the meatloaf from the oven and place onto a wire rack to cool slightly.
7. Cut the meatloaf into desired sized slices and serve warm.

Nutritional Information per Serving

Calories: 422

Fat: 27.8g

Sat Fat: 9.2g

Cholesterol: 178mg

Sodium: 792mg

Carbohydrates: 2.3g

Fiber: 0.2g

Sugar: 0.3g

Protein: 44g

Meat Recipes

Beef with Mushroom Gravy

A healthy and hearty choice for dinner meals... Even mushroom haters would love to enjoy this hearty, creamy mushroom sauce alongside the beef.

Yield: 4 servings

Preparation time: 20 minutes

Cooking time: 20 minutes

Allergens: dairy

Ingredients:

For Mushroom Gravy:

- 4 bacon slices, chopped
- 3 tablespoons butter
- 3 garlic cloves, minced
- 1 teaspoon dried thyme
- 1½ cups fresh button mushrooms, sliced
- Salt and ground black pepper, as required
- 7 ounces cream cheese
- ½ cup heavy cream

For Steak:

- 4 (6-ounce) grass-fed beef tenderloin filets
- Salt and ground black pepper, as required
- 3 tablespoons butter

Instructions:

1. For mushroom gravy: heat a large nonstick skillet over medium-high heat and cook the bacon for about 8-10 minutes.
2. Place the bacon onto a paper towel-lined plate to drain.
3. Discard the bacon grease from the skillet.
4. In the same skillet, melt the butter over medium heat and sauté garlic and thyme for about 1 minute.

5. Add the mushrooms, salt, and black pepper and cook for about 5-7 minutes, stirring frequently.
6. Lower the heat and stir in the cream cheese until smooth.
7. Stir in the cream and cook for about 2-3 minutes or until heated completely.
8. Meanwhile, rub the beef filets with the salt and black pepper evenly.
9. In a large cast iron skillet, melt the butter over medium heat and cook the filets for about 5-7 minutes per side.
10. Remove the skillet of mushroom gravy from the heat and stir in the bacon,
11. Place the filets onto serving plates and serve with the topping of mushroom gravy.

Nutritional Information per Serving
Calories: 895
Fat: 67.9g
Sat Fat: 35.2g
Cholesterol: 309mg
Sodium: 1048mg
Carbohydrates: 3.9g
Fiber: 0.4g
Sugar: 0.6g
Protein: 65.2g

Creamy & Cheesy Steak

Tender steak with a savory and mildly spicy creamy sauce...
This rich and creamy sauce enhances the taste of steak.

Yield: 4 servings

Preparation time: 15 minutes

Cooking time: 1 hour

Allergens: dairy

Ingredients:

- 4 cups heavy cream
- 3 tablespoons Parmesan cheese, shredded
- 3 ounces Gorgonzola cheese, crumbled
- 1/8 teaspoon ground nutmeg
- Salt and ground black pepper, as required
- Pinch of onion powder
- Pinch of garlic powder
- Pinch of lemon pepper
- 4 (8-ounce) grass-fed beef tenderloin steaks

Instructions:

1. In a pan, add the heavy cream over medium heat and bring to a boil.
2. Then, reduce heat to low and let it cook one hour, stirring occasionally.
3. Meanwhile, in a small bowl, mix together onion powder, garlic powder, lemon pepper, salt, and black pepper.
4. Sprinkle the steaks with seasoning mixture evenly.
5. Preheat the outdoor grill to medium-high heat. Grease the grill grate.
6. Grill the steaks for about 4-5 minutes from both sides or until desired doneness.
7. Remove the pan of cream from heat and immediately, stir in cheeses, nutmeg, salt, and black pepper until well combined.
8. Place the steaks onto serving plates and serve alongside the creamy sauce evenly.

Nutritional Information per Serving
Calories: 925
Fat: 65.6g
Sat Fat: 37.6g
Cholesterol: 390mg
Sodium: 563mg

Carbohydrates: 5g

Fiber: 0.7g

Sugar: 0.2g

Protein: 77.4g

Steak with Blueberry Sauce

An astonishingly good recipe for steak with butter, ginger and soy sauce... Stir-fried beef steak is simmered in the sauce for a flavorful dish.

Yield: 4 servings

Preparation time: 15 minutes

Cooking time: 15 minutes

Allergens: dairy

Ingredients:

For Sauce:

- 2 tablespoons butter
- 2 tablespoons yellow onion, chopped
- 2 garlic cloves, minced
- 1 teaspoon fresh thyme, chopped finely
- 1 1/3 cups homemade beef broth
- 2 tablespoons fresh lemon juice
- ¾ cup fresh blueberries

For Steak:

- 2 tablespoons butter

- 4 (6-ounce) grass-fed flank steaks
- Salt and ground black pepper, as required

Instructions:

1. For sauce: in a pan, melt the butter over medium heat and sauté the onion for about 2 minutes.
2. Add the garlic and thyme and sauté for about 1 minute.
3. Stir in the broth and bring to a gentle simmer.
4. Reduce heat to low and cook for about 10 minutes.
5. Meanwhile, for steak: in a skillet, melt the butter over medium-high heat and cook steaks with salt and black pepper for about 3-4 minutes per side.
6. With a slotted spoon, transfer the steak onto the serving plates.
7. Add the sauce in the skillet and stir to scrape up the brown bits from the bottom.
8. Stir in the lemon juice, blueberries, salt, and black pepper and cook for about 1-2 minutes.
9. Remove from the heat and place the blueberry sauce over the steaks.
10. Serve immediately.

Nutritional Information per Serving

Calories: 467

Fat: 24.3g

Sat Fat: 13.4g

Cholesterol: 123mg

Sodium: 473mg

Carbohydrates: 5.5g

Fiber: 0.9g

Sugar: 3.3g

Protein: 49.5g

Beef Curry

When it comes to a satisfying meals, beef curry is at the top of the list... Curry of tender meat and fragrant curry paste comes on the dinner table in just 40 minutes.

Yield: 8 servings

Preparation time: 15 minutes

Cooking time: 3 hours 10 minutes

Allergens: dairy

Ingredients:

- 2½ pounds grass-fed beef chuck roast, cubed into 1-inch size
- 2 tablespoons butter
- 3 tablespoons Thai red curry paste
- 2½ cups unsweetened coconut milk
- ½ cup homemade chicken broth
- Salt and ground black pepper, as required
- ¼ cup fresh cilantro, chopped

Instructions:

1. In a large pan, melt butter over low heat and sauté the curry paste for about 4-5 minutes.
2. Stir in the coconut milk and broth and bring to a gentle simmer, stirring occasionally.
3. Simmer for about 4-5 minutes.
4. Stir in beef and gain bring to a boil over medium heat.
5. Reduce heat to low and cook covered for about 2½ hours, stirring occasionally
6. Remove from the heat and with a slotted spoon, transfer the beef into a bowl.
7. Set the pan of curry aside for about 10 minutes.
8. With a slotted spoon, remove the fats from top of the curry.
9. Return the pan over medium heat.

10. Stir in cooked beef and bring to a gentle simmer.

11. Reduce the heat to low and cook, uncovered for about 30 minutes or until desired thickness.

12. Stir in salt and remove from heat.

13. Serve hot with the garnishing of cilantro.

Nutritional Information per Serving

Calories: 753

Fat: 63.6g

Sat Fat: 33.6g

Cholesterol: 154mg

Sodium: 190mg

Carbohydrates: 5.8g

Fiber: 1.7g

Sugar: 2.6g

Protein: 39.4g

Beef Chili

An authentic Mexican style beef chili recipe.... This beef chili recipe will win the heart of pickiest eaters too.

Yield: 8 servings

Preparation time: 15 minutes

Cooking time: 3 hours 10 minutes

Allergens: dairy

Ingredients:

- 2 pounds grass-fed ground beef
- 1 yellow onion, chopped
- ½ cup green bell pepper, seeded and chopped
- ½ cup carrot, peeled and chopped
- 4 ounces fresh mushrooms, sliced
- 2 garlic cloves, minced
- 1 (6-ounce) can sugar-free tomato paste
- 2 tablespoons red chili powder
- 1 tablespoon ground cumin
- 1 teaspoon ground cinnamon
- 1 teaspoon red pepper flakes, crushed
- ½ teaspoon ground allspice

- Salt and ground black pepper, as required
- 4 cups water
- 1 cup sour cream

Instructions:

1. Heat a large non-stick pan over medium-high heat and cook beef for about 8-10 minutes.
2. Drain the excess grease from the pan.
3. Stir in remaining ingredients except for sour cream and bring the mixture to a boil.
4. Reduce heat to medium-low and let it cook covered for about 3 hours.
5. Serve hot with the topping of sour cream.

Nutritional Information per Serving

Calories: 315

Fat: 13.8g

Sat Fat: 6.5g

Cholesterol: 114mg

Sodium: 90mg

Carbohydrates: 10.3g

Fiber: 2.6g

Sugar: 4.4g

Protein: 37.4g

Shepherd Pie

Here's a healthier take on family favorite with definitive version... This version features ground beef with a crown of mashed cauliflower for a topping.

Yield: 6 servings

Preparation time: 20 minutes

Cooking time: 50 minutes

Allergens: dairy

Ingredients:

- ¼ cup olive oil
- 1 pound grass-fed ground beef
- ½ cup celery, chopped
- ¼ cup yellow onion, chopped
- 3 garlic cloves, minced
- 1 cup tomatoes, chopped
- 2 (12-ounce) packages riced cauliflower, cooked and well drained
- 1 cup Cheddar cheese, shredded
- ¼ cup Parmesan cheese, shredded
- 1 cup heavy cream

- 1 teaspoon dried thyme

Instructions:

1. Preheat your oven to 350° F (180° C).
2. Heat oil in a large skillet over medium and cook the ground beef, celery, onions, and garlic for about 8-10 minutes.
3. Remove from the heat and drain the excess grease.
4. Immediately, stir in the tomatoes.
5. Transfer mixture into a 10x7-inch casserole dish evenly.
6. In a food processor, add the cauliflower, cheeses, cream and thyme and pulse until mashed potatoes like a mixture is formed.
7. Spread the cauliflower mixture over the meat in the casserole dish evenly.
8. Bake for about 35-40 mins.
9. Remove from the oven and let it cool slightly before serving.
10. Cut into desired sized pieces and serve.

Nutritional Information per Serving

Calories: 411

Fat: 27.9g

Sat Fat: 12.2g

Cholesterol: 117mg
Sodium: 274mg
Carbohydrates: 9g
Fiber: 3.5g
Sugar: 4g
Protein: 32g

Beef Crust Pizza

An excellent alternative to traditional dough pizza... Without a doubt, this crustless pizza tastes as good as it looks.

Yield: 8 servings

Preparation time: 15 minutes

Cooking time: 23 minutes

Allergens: egg, dairy

Ingredients:

- 2 pounds grass-fed lean ground beef
- ½ cup Parmesan cheese, grated
- 2 organic eggs
- 2 teaspoons Italian seasoning
- 1 teaspoon garlic powder
- Salt and ground black pepper, as required
- 9 ounces cooked spinach, chopped
- 2 tomatoes, sliced
- 2 cups mozzarella cheese, shredded

Instructions:

1. Preheat your oven to 450° F (230° C).
2. In a bowl, add beef, parmesan cheese, eggs, Italian seasoning, garlic powder, salt, and black pepper and mix until well combined.
3. Place beef mixture onto a large baking sheet in a circle with slight sides.
4. Bake for about 20 minutes.
5. Remove from the oven and carefully, discard excess grease from baking sheet.
6. Arrange spinach and tomato slices on top of beef mixture and sprinkle with the mozzarella cheese.
7. Now, set oven to broiler on high.
8. Broil for about 2-3 minutes.
9. Cut into 8 equal sized wedges and serve.

Nutritional Information per Serving

Calories: 282

Fat: 11.1g

Sat Fat: 4.5g

Cholesterol: 151mg

Sodium: 208mg

Carbohydrates: 3.1g

Fiber: 1.1g

Sugar: 1.2g

Protein: 4.1g

Beef Stuffed Bell Peppers

A restaurant-style dish that can be easily prepared at home...Ground beef and mushrooms help these bell peppers to become a great meal for a weeknight dinner.

Yield: 6 servings

Preparation time: 15 minutes

Cooking time: 15 minutes

Allergens: dairy

Ingredients:

- 1 pound grass-fed ground beef
- 1 garlic clove, minced
- 2 teaspoons coconut oil
- 1 cup white mushrooms, chopped
- 1 cup yellow onion, chopped
- 1 tablespoon red chili powder
- 1 tablespoon ground cumin
- ¼ teaspoon ground cinnamon
- Salt, to taste
- ½ cup homemade tomato puree
- 3 large bell peppers, halved lengthwise and cored

- 1 cup water
- 4 ounces sharp cheddar cheese, shredded

Instructions:

1. In a skillet, heat oil over medium-high and sauté garlic for about 30 seconds.
2. Add beef and cook for about 5 minutes, crumbling with the spoon.
3. Add mushrooms and onion and cook for about 5-6 minutes.
4. Stir in spices and cook for about 30 seconds.
5. Remove from heat and stir in tomato puree.
6. Meanwhile, in a microwave-safe dish, arrange the bell peppers, cut-side down.
7. Pour water in baking dish.
8. With a plastic wrap, cover the baking dish and microwave on High for about 4-5 minutes.
9. Remove from microwave and uncover the baking dish.
10. Dain the water completely
11. Now in the baking dish, arrange the bell peppers cut-side up.
12. Stuff the bell peppers with beef mixture evenly and top with cheese.
13. Microwave on High for about 2-3 minutes.

14. Serve warm.

Nutritional Information per Serving
Calories: 275
Fat: 13.2g
Sat Fat: 7.2g
Cholesterol: 87mg
Sodium: 219mg
Carbohydrates: 10g
Fiber: 2.3g
Sugar: 5.2g
Protein: 29.5g

Pork & Spinach Loaf

A flavorful baked feast for family and friend's gatherings... Surely everyone would love to enjoy these wonderful flavors.

Yield: 8 servings

Preparation time: 15 minutes

Cooking time: 1¼ hours

Allergens: egg, dairy

Ingredients:

- 1 pound ground pork
- 1 pound grass-fed lean ground beef
- ½ cup yellow onion, chopped
- ½ cup green bell pepper, seeded and chopped
- 2 garlic cloves, minced
- 1 cup cheddar cheese, grated
- ¼ cup sugar-free ketchup
- ¼ cup sugar-free HP steak sauce
- 2 organic eggs, beaten
- 1 teaspoon dried thyme, crushed
- Salt and ground black pepper, as required
- 3 cups fresh spinach, chopped
- 2 cups mozzarella cheese, grated freshly

Instructions:

1. Preheat your oven to 350° F (180° C). Lightly. Grease a baking dish.
2. In a large bowl, add all ingredients except for spinach and mozzarella cheese and mix until well combined.
3. Place a large wax paper onto a smooth surface.
4. Place the meat mixture over wax paper.

5. Place the spinach over meat mixture, pressing slightly.
6. Top with the mozzarella cheese evenly.
7. Roll the wax paper around meat mixture to form a meatloaf.
8. Carefully, remove the wax paper and place the meatloaf onto the prepared baking dish.
9. Bake for about 1-1¼ hours.
10. Remove from oven and set it aside for about 10 minutes before serving.
11. With a sharp knife cut into desired slices and serve.

Nutritional Information per Serving

Calories: 300

Fat: 14.1g

Sat Fat: 7g

Cholesterol: 138mg

Sodium: 323mg

Carbohydrates: 6.6g

Fiber: 0.7g

Sugar: 4g

Protein: 34g

Pork Chops in Rosemary Sauce

A hit recipe of pork chops for the family and friend's dinner table... These fabulous pork chops are so delicious.

Yield: 4 servings

Preparation time: 15 minutes

Cooking time: 35 minutes

Allergens: dairy

Ingredients:

- 1 tablespoon olive oil
- 4 large boneless rib pork chops
- 1 teaspoon salt
- 1 cup cremini mushrooms, chopped roughly
- 3 tablespoons onion, chopped finely
- 2 tablespoons fresh rosemary, chopped
- 1/3 cup homemade chicken broth
- 1 tablespoon Dijon mustard
- 1 tablespoon unsalted butter
- 2/3 cup heavy cream
- 2 tablespoons sour cream

Instructions:

1. Heat the oil in a large skillet over medium and sear the chops with the salt for about 3-4 minutes or until browned completely.
2. With a slotted spoon, transfer the pork chops onto a plate and set aside.
3. In the same skillet, add the mushrooms, onion, and rosemary and sauté for about 3 minutes.
4. Stir in the cooked chops, broth and bring the mixture to a boil.
5. Reduce the heat to low and cook, covered for about 20 minutes.
6. With a slotted spoon, transfer the pork chops onto a plate and set aside.
7. In the skillet, stir in the butter until melted.
8. Add the heavy cream and sour cream and stir until smooth.
9. Stir in the cooked pork chops and cook for about 2-3 minutes or until heated completely.
10. Serve hot.

Nutritional Information per Serving

Calories: 400

Fat: 21.6g

Sat Fat: 9.9g

Cholesterol: 162mg
Sodium: 820mg
Carbohydrates: 3.6g
Fiber: 1.1g
Sugar: 0.8g
Protein: 46.3g

Stuffed Leg of Lamb

A roasted leg of lamb with the stuffing of kale, olives, and feta cheese... This stuffed leg of lamb will be a great choice for special occasion's dinners.

Yield: 12 servings

Preparation time: 15 minutes

Cooking time: 1 hour 40 minutes

Allergens: dairy

Ingredients:

- 1/3 cup fresh parsley, minced finely
- 8 garlic cloves, minced and divided
- 3 tablespoons olive oil, divided
- Salt and ground black pepper, as required
- 1 (4-pound) grass-fed boneless leg of lamb, butterflied and trimmed
- 1/3 cup yellow onion, minced
- 1 bunch fresh kale, trimmed and chopped
- ½ cup Kalamata olives, pitted and chopped
- ½ cup feta cheese, crumbled
- 1 teaspoon fresh lemon zest, grated finely

Instructions:

1. In a large bowl, add the parsley, 4 garlic cloves, 2 tablespoons of oil, salt and black pepper and mix until well combined.
2. Add leg of lamb and coat with parsley mixture generously. Set aside at room temperature.
3. In a large skillet, heat remaining oil over medium heat and sauté the onion and remaining garlic for about 4-5 minutes.
4. Add the kale and cook for about 4-5 minutes.
5. Remove from the heat and set aside to cool for at least 10 minutes.
6. Stir in remaining ingredients.
7. Preheat your oven to 450° F (230° C). Grease a shallow roasting pan.
8. Place the leg of lamb onto a smooth surface, cut-side up.
9. Place the kale mixture in the center, leaving 1-inch border from both sides.
10. Roll the short side to seal the stuffing and with a kitchen string tightly, tie the roll at many places.
11. Arrange the roll into the prepared roasting pan, seam-side down.
12. Roast for about 15 minutes.
13. Now, reduce temperature of oven to 350° F (180° C).

14. Roast for about 1-1¼ hours.

15. Remove the lamb from oven and set aside for about 10-20 minutes before slicing.

16. With a sharp knife, cut the roll into desired size slices and serve.

Nutritional Information per Serving

Calories: 345

Fat: 16.5g

Sat Fat: 5.5g

Cholesterol: 142mg

Sodium: 251mg

Carbohydrates: 2.9g

Fiber: 0.5g

Sugar: 0.4g

Protein: 44g

Broiled Lamb Chops

One of the quickest way to prepare lamb chops... Fresh lemon and thyme complement the flavor of lamb chops in a wonderful way.

Yield: 4 servings

Preparation time: 15 minutes

Cooking time: 8 minutes

Allergens: dairy

Ingredients:

- 2 tablespoons garlic, minced
- 2 tablespoons fresh oregano, minced
- ½ teaspoon fresh lemon zest, grated finely
- 1 tablespoon olive oil
- 2 tablespoons fresh lemon juice
- Salt and ground black pepper, as required
- 8 (4-ounce) grass-fed lamb loin chops, trimmed
- 2 tablespoons Parmesan cheese, shredded

Instructions:

1. In a large bowl, add all ingredients except for lamb chops and Parmesan and mix until well combined.
2. Add the chops and coat with garlic mixture generously.
3. Cover and refrigerate to marinate for one hour or more.
4. Preheat the broiler of the oven to high heat. Grease a broiler pan.
5. Arrange the chops onto the broiler pan.
6. Broil for about 3-4 minutes per side.
7. Serve hot with the sprinkling of the Parmesan.

Nutritional Information per Serving

Calories: 477

Fat: 21.1g

Sat Fat: 7g

Cholesterol: 206mg

Sodium: 256mg

Carbohydrates: 3.1g

Fiber: 1.1g

Sugar: 0.3g

Protein: 65.2g

Fish & Seafood Recipes

Grouper Curry

An Asian style fish curry with awesome spicy flavor... This awesome fish curry will go down great at any dinner party.

Yield: 6 servings

Preparation time: 15 minutes

Cooking time: 15 minutes

Allergens: absent

Ingredients:

- 1 tablespoon coconut oil
- 1 small yellow onion, chopped
- 2 garlic cloves, minced
- 1 teaspoon fresh ginger, minced
- 1 large tomato, peeled and chopped
- 1½ tablespoons red curry paste
- ¼ cup water
- 1¼ cups unsweetened coconut milk
- 1½ pounds skinless grouper fillets, cubed into 2-inch size
- Salt, to taste
- 2 tablespoons fresh basil leaves, chopped

Instructions:

1. In a large skillet, melt the coconut oil over medium heat and sauté the onion, garlic, and ginger for about 5 minutes.
2. Add the tomatoes and cook for about 2-3 minutes, crushing with the back of the spoon.
3. Add the curry paste and sauté for about 2 minutes.
4. Add the water and coconut milk and bring to a gentle boil.
5. Stir in grouper pieces and cook for about 4-5 minutes.
6. Stir in the salt and basil leaves and serve hot.

Nutritional Information per Serving

Calories: 307

Fat: 18g

Sat Fat: 12.9g

Cholesterol: 53mg

Sodium: 97mg

Carbohydrates: 6.7g

Fiber: 1.8g

Sugar: 3g

Protein: 30g

Cheesy Salmon

An Omega 3 rich and super delicious salmon in a balanced cheesy and creamy sauce... Mustard and lemon juice balance this rich sauce nicely.

Yield: 8 servings

Preparation time: 15 minutes

Cooking time: 23 minutes

Allergens: dairy

Ingredients:

- 1/3 cup mayonnaise
- 2 garlic cloves, minced
- 2 tablespoons fresh lemon juice
- 1 tablespoon Dijon mustard
- 2 pounds salmon fillets
- 1 large yellow onion, sliced thinly
- Salt and ground black pepper, as required
- ¼ cup Parmesan cheese, shredded finely
- ½ cup Mozzarella cheese, shredded finely

Instructions:

1. Preheat your oven to 400° F (200° C). Line a rimmed baking sheet with a foil.
2. In a small bowl, add the mayonnaise, lemon juice, mustard and garlic, and mix until well combined.
3. Arrange the salmon fillets onto the prepared baking sheet and sprinkle with salt and pepper.
4. Place the onion slices over the salmon fillets evenly, followed by the mayonnaise mixture and cheeses.
5. Bake for about 15-18 minutes.
6. Now, set the oven to broiler.
7. Broil the salmon fillets for about 2-5 minutes.

Nutritional Information per Serving

Calories: 214

Fat: 11.4g

Sat Fat: 2.1g

Cholesterol: 55mg

Sodium: 216mg

Carbohydrates: 4.7g

Fiber: 0.5g

Sugar: 1.5g

Protein: 23.9g

Salmon with Salsa

A wonderful and healthier weeknight dinner meal with a touch of elegance... Surely this pan-seared salmon compliments avocado salsa in a delish way.

Yield: 4 servings

Preparation time: 15 minutes

Cooking time: 8 minutes

Allergens: dairy

Ingredients:

For Salsa:

- 2 large ripe avocados, peeled, pitted and cut into small chunks
- 1 small tomato, chopped
- 2 tablespoons red onion, chopped finely
- ¼ cup fresh cilantro, chopped finely
- 1 tablespoon jalapeño pepper, seeded and minced finely
- 1 garlic clove, minced finely
- 3 tablespoons fresh lime juice
- Salt and ground black pepper, as required

For Salmon:

- 4 (5-ounce) (1-inch thick) salmon fillets
- Sea salt and freshly ground black pepper, as required
- 3 tablespoons butter
- 1 tablespoon fresh rosemary leaves, chopped
- 1 tablespoon fresh lemon juice

Instructions:

1. For salsa: Add all ingredients in a bowl and gently, stir to combine.
2. With a plastic wrap, cover the bowl and refrigerate before serving.
3. For salmon: season each salmon fillet with salt and black pepper generously.
4. In a large skillet, melt butter over medium-high.
5. Place the salmon fillets, skins side up and cook for about 4 minutes.
6. Carefully change the side of each salmon fillet and cook for about 4 minutes more.
7. Stir in the rosemary and lemon juice and remove from the heat.
8. Divide the salsa onto serving plates evenly.
9. To each plate with 1 salmon fillet and serve.

Nutritional Information per Serving

Calories: 481

Fat: 37.2g

Sat Fat: 10.9g

Cholesterol: 85mg

Sodium: 172mg

Carbohydrates: 11g

Fiber: 7.6g

Sugar: 1.5g

Protein: 29.9g

Salmon & Veggie Parcel

Discover an aromatic salmon and vegetable surprise in this dinner recipe... Bell peppers, tomatoes, parsley and lemon juice pair nicely with Omega-3 rich salmon.

Yield: 6 servings

Preparation time: 15 minutes

Cooking time: 20 minutes

Allergens: absent

Ingredients:

- 6 (3-ounce) salmon fillets
- Salt and ground black pepper, as required
- 1 yellow bell pepper, seeded and cubed
- 1 red bell pepper, seeded and cubed
- 4 plum tomatoes, cubed
- 1 small yellow onion, sliced thinly
- ½ cup fresh parsley, chopped
- ¼ cup olive oil
- 2 tablespoons fresh lemon juice

Instructions:

1. Preheat your oven to 400° F (200° C).
2. Arrange 6 pieces of foil onto a smooth surface.
3. Place 1 salmon fillet onto each foil paper and sprinkle with salt and black pepper.
4. In a bowl, add the bell peppers, tomato and onion, and mix.
5. Place veggie mixture over each fillet evenly and top with parsley and capers.
6. Drizzle with oil and lemon juice.
7. Fold the foil around salmon mixture to seal it.
8. Arrange the foil packets onto a large baking sheet in a single layer.
9. Bake for about 20 minutes.
10. Serve hot.

Nutritional Information per Serving

Calories: 224

Fat: 14g

Sat Fat: 2g

Cholesterol: 38mg

Sodium: 811mg

Carbohydrates: 8.7g

Fiber: 1.9g

Sugar: 5.9g

Protein: 18.2g

Tilapia is broiled with the coating of parmesan cheese, mayonnaise, and butter for an impressive meal. Fresh lemon juice adds a light, zingy touch in the creamy and cheesy coating.

Yield: 8 servings

Preparation time: 10 minutes

Cooking time: 5 minutes

Allergens: dairy

Ingredients:

- 2 pounds tilapia fillets
- ½ cup Parmesan cheese, grated
- 3 tablespoons mayonnaise
- ¼ cup unsalted butter, softened
- 2 tablespoons fresh lemon juice
- ¼ teaspoon dried thyme, crushed
- Salt and ground black pepper, as required

Instructions:

1. Preheat your oven to broiler on high. Grease the broiler pan.
2. In a large bowl, mix all ingredients together except for tilapia fillets. Set aside.
3. Place the fillets onto prepared broiler pan in a single layer.
4. Broil the fillets for about 2-3 minutes.
5. Remove from oven and top the fillets with cheese mixture evenly.
6. Broil for about 2 minutes further.

Nutritional Information per Serving
Calories: 185
Fat: 9.8g
Sat Fat: 5g
Cholesterol: 76mg
Sodium: 183mg
Carbohydrates: 1.4g
Fiber: 0g
Sugar: 0.4g
Protein: 23.2g

Cod & Veggies Bake

An effortless way to make a superb tasting combo of healthy cod fish, fresh vegetables and feta cheese... Your family would love to enjoy this meal so much.

Yield: 4 servings

Preparation time: 15 minutes

Cooking time: 20 minutes

Allergens: dairy

Ingredients:

- 1 teaspoon olive oil
- ½ cup onion, minced
- 1 cup zucchini, chopped
- 1 garlic clove, minced
- 2 tablespoons fresh basil, chopped
- 2 cups fresh tomatoes, chopped
- Salt and ground black pepper, as required
- 4 (6-ounce) cod steaks
- 1/3 cup feta cheese, crumbled

Instructions:

1. Preheat your oven to 450° F (230°C). Grease a large shallow baking dish.
2. In a skillet, heat oil over medium and sauté the onion, zucchini, and garlic for about 4-5 minutes.
3. Stir in the basil, tomatoes, salt, and black pepper and immediately remove from heat.
4. Place the cod steaks into the prepared baking dish in a single layer and top with tomato mixture evenly.
5. Sprinkle with the cheese evenly.
6. Bake for 15 minutes or until desired doneness.
7. Serve hot.

Nutritional Information per Serving

Calories: 250

Fat: 5.5g

Sat Fat: 24g

Cholesterol: 105mg

Sodium: 319mg

Carbohydrates: 6.6g

Fiber: 1.7g

Sugar: 4g

Protein: 42g

Baked Trout

A very simple recipe that turns the whole trout in a delicious dinner treat... The combo of fresh butter, dill and lemon juice gives trout a really refreshing touch.

Yield: 6 servings

Preparation time: 15 minutes

Cooking time: 25 minutes

Allergens: dairy

Ingredients:

- 2 (1½-pound) wild-caught trout, gutted and cleaned
- Salt and ground black pepper, as required
- 1 lemon, sliced
- 2 tablespoons fresh dill, minced
- 2 tablespoons butter, melted
- 2 tablespoons fresh lemon juice

Instructions:

1. Preheat your oven to 475° F (240° C). Arrange a wire rack onto a foil-lined baking sheet.
2. Sprinkle the trout with salt and pepper from inside and outside generously.
3. Fill the fish cavity with lemon slices and dill
4. Place the trout onto the prepared baking sheet and drizzle with the melted butter and lemon juice.
5. Bake for about 25 minutes.
6. Serve hot.

Nutritional Information per Serving

Calories: 469

Fat: 23.1g

Sat Fat: 5.8g

Cholesterol: 178mg

Sodium: 210mg

Carbohydrates: 0.9g

Fiber: 0.2g

Sugar: 0.2g

Protein: 60.7g

Fish Taco Bowl

An amazing combo of white fish and cabbage with delicious and aromatic spices... Creamy and spicy dressing pairs nicely with fish and veggies.

Yield: 6 servings

Preparation time: 20 minutes

Cooking time: 8 minutes

Allergens: dairy

Ingredients:

For Taco Bowl:

- 2 teaspoons fish rub
- 1 teaspoon ground cumin
- ½ teaspoon red chili powder
- 3 (8-ounce) white fish fillets, pat dried
- 4 teaspoons olive oil, divided
- 1 medium green cabbage head, sliced thinly
- ½ medium red cabbage head, sliced thinly
- ½ cup scallions, sliced thinly and divided

For Dressing:

- ½ cup mayonnaise
- 2 tablespoons fresh lime juice
- 2 teaspoons green Tabasco sauce
- Salt, to taste

Instructions:

1. In a bowl, add the fish rub, cumin, and chili powder.
2. Coat the fish fillets with 2 teaspoons of oil and then, rub with the spice mixture.
3. In a heavy frying pan, heat the remaining olive oil over medium-high heat and cook fish fillets for about 4 minutes per side or until desired doneness.
4. Meanwhile, in a large bowl, add the cabbage and ¼ cup of the scallion and mix.
5. For dressing: in another bowl, add all the ingredients and beat until smooth.
6. Pour about ¾ of the dressing over cabbage mixture and gently, stir to combine.
7. Remove fish from the heat and transfer onto a cutting board to cool slightly.
8. With 2 forks, shred the fish fillets.
9. Divide the cabbage mixture into the bowls and top with fish, followed by remaining scallions.
10. Drizzle with remaining dressing and serve immediately.

Nutritional Information per Serving

Calories: 399

Fat: 24.9g

Sat Fat: 3.9g

Cholesterol: 94mg

Sodium: 534mg

Carbohydrates: 11.3g

Fiber: 4.8g

Sugar: 5.9g

Protein: 30.9g

Scallops with Broccoli

The flavors of this dish of scallops and broccoli are simple but superb as well... This dish will be welcomed nicely at a special gathering dinner.

Yield: 5 servings

Preparation time: 15 minutes

Cooking time: 5 minutes

Allergens: dairy

Ingredients:

For Broccoli:

- 1¼ pounds small broccoli florets
- 2 tablespoons unsalted butter, melted

For Scallops:

- 1 tablespoon butter
- 2 garlic cloves, minced
- 1 pound fresh jumbo scallops, rinsed and pat dried
- Salt and ground black pepper, as required
- 2 tablespoons fresh lemon juice
- 2 scallions (green part), sliced thinly

Instructions:

1. For broccoli: arrange a steamer basket in a pan of water and bring to a boil.
2. Place broccoli in steamer basket and steam, covered for about 4-5 minutes.
3. Meanwhile, in a large skillet, melt the butter over medium-high heat and sauté the garlic for about 1 minute.
4. Add the scallops and cook 2 minutes per side.
5. Stir in the salt, black pepper, and lemon juice and remove from heat.
6. Drain broccoli and drizzle with oil evenly.
7. Divide the coked broccoli onto serving plates and top with scallops evenly.
8. Serve immediately with the garnishing of scallion.

Nutritional Information per Serving

Calories: 221

Fat: 10g

Sat Fat: 5.6g

Cholesterol: 60mg

Sodium: 323mg

Carbohydrates: 11.4g

Fiber: 3.2g

Sugar: 2.3g
Protein: 22.6g

Shrimp with Zucchini Pasta

A restaurant quality dinner dish that is super-quick to prepare with a wonderful taste... Pan seared shrimp and spiralized zucchini pasta marry each other nicely.

Yield: 4 servings

Preparation time: 15 minutes

Cooking time: 6 minutes

Allergens: dairy

Ingredients:

- 2 tablespoons unsalted butter
- 1 large garlic clove, minced
- ¼ teaspoon red pepper flakes, crushed
- 1 pound medium shrimp, peeled and deveined
- Salt and ground black pepper, as required
- 1/3 cup homemade chicken broth
- 2 medium zucchinis, spiralized with blade C
- 1 tablespoon fresh parsley, chopped finely

Instructions:

1. Heat oil in a large skillet over medium heat and sauté garlic and red pepper flakes for about 1 minute.
2. Add shrimp and black pepper and cook for about 1 minute per side.
3. Add broth and zucchini noodles and cook for about 3-4 minutes.
4. Garnish with parsley and serve hot.

Nutritional Information per Serving

Calories: 206

Fat: 8g

Sat Fat: 4.3g

Cholesterol: 254mg

Sodium: 392mg

Carbohydrates: 5.5g

Fiber: 1.2g

Sugar: 1.8g

Protein: 27.6g

Shrimp in Creamy Sauce

A wonderfully delicious supper of shrimp that is really easy to cook... Shrimp are simmered in a delish sauce of cream, cheese and curry powdered for a nice meal.

Yield: 3 servings

Preparation time: 20 minutes

Cooking time: 15 minutes

Allergens: egg, dairy, nuts

Ingredients:

For Shrimp:

- ½ounce Parmigiano Reggiano, grated
- 1 large organic egg
- 2 tablespoons almond flour
- ½ teaspoon organic baking powder
- ¼ teaspoon curry powder
- 1 tablespoon water
- 12 medium shrimp, peeled and deveined
- 3 tablespoons unsalted butter

For Creamy Sauce:

- 2 tablespoons unsalted butter
- ½ of small yellow onion, chopped
- 1 garlic clove, chopped finely
- 2 Thai red chilies, sliced
- ½ teaspoon curry powder
- ½ cup heavy cream
- 1/3 cup cheddar cheese, grated
- Salt and ground black pepper, as required

Instructions:

1. For shrimp: in a bowl, add all ingredients except the shrimp and butter and mix until well.
2. Add the shrimp and coat with the cheese mixture generously.
3. In a pan, melt the butter over medium heat and stir fry the shrimp for about 3-4 minutes or until golden brown from all sides.
4. With a slotted spoon, transfer the shrimp onto a plate.
5. For sauce: in another pan, melt the butter over medium-low heat and sauté the onion for about 3-5 minutes.
6. Add the garlic, chilies and curry powder and sauté for about 1 minute.

7. Reduce heat to low and stir in the heavy cream and cheddar until well combined.
8. Cook for about 1-2 minutes, stirring continuously.
9. Add the cooked shrimps and stir to combine.
10. Serve immediately.

Nutritional Information per Serving

Calories: 472

Fat: 37.7g

Sat Fat: 21.5g

Cholesterol: 343mg

Sodium: 541mg

Carbohydrates: 5.4g

Fiber: 1g

Sugar: 1.1g

Protein: 29.1g

Cheesy Shrimp Bake

The main course baked meal with superb flavors... This baked shrimp casserole will be a great choice to impress a crowd or company at the dinner table.

Yield: 6 servings

Preparation time: 15 minutes

Cooking time: 30 minutes

Allergens: dairy

Ingredients:

- ¼ cup unsalted butter
- 1 tablespoon garlic, minced
- 1½ pounds large shrimp, peeled and deveined
- ¾ teaspoon dried oregano, crushed
- ¼ teaspoon red pepper flakes, crushed
- ¼ cup fresh parsley, chopped
- ¾ cup dry vermouth
- 1 (14½-ounce) can sugar-free diced tomatoes, drained
- 4 ounces feta cheese, crumbled

Instructions:

1. Preheat your oven to 350° F (180° C).
2. In a large skillet, melt butter over medium-high heat.
3. Add the garlic and sauté for about 1 minute.
4. Add the shrimp, oregano and red pepper flakes and cook for about 4-5 minutes.
5. Stir in the parsley and salt and immediately transfer into a casserole dish evenly.
6. In the same skillet, add vermouth on medium heat. Simmer for about 2-3 minutes or until liquid reduces to half.
7. Stir in tomatoes and cook for about 2-3 minutes.

8. Pour the tomato mixture over shrimp mixture evenly.
9. Top with cheese evenly.
10. Bake for about 15-20 minutes or until the top becomes golden brown.
11. Remove from the oven and serve hot.

Nutritional Information per Serving

Calories: 250

Fat: 11.9g

Sat Fat: 7.7g

Cholesterol: 199mg

Sodium: 414mg

Carbohydrates: 7.1g

Fiber: 1g

Sugar: 2.9g

Protein: 24.8g

Vegetarian Recipes

Spinach in Creamy Sauce

A really simple and quickest recipe that prepares a delicious and elegant spinach dish… Fresh lemon juice and cream cheese give spinach a refreshingly creamy touch.

Yield: 4 servings

Preparation time: 10 minutes

Cooking time: 15 minutes

Allergens: dairy

Ingredients:

- 2 tablespoons unsalted butter
- 1 medium yellow onion, chopped
- 1 cup cream cheese, softened
- 2 (10-ounce) packages frozen spinach, thawed & squeezed dry
- 2-3 tablespoons water
- Salt and ground black pepper, as required
- 2 teaspoons fresh lemon juice

Instructions:

1. In a skillet, melt butter over medium heat and sauté the onion for about 6-8 minutes.
2. Add the cream cheese and cook for about 2 minutes or until melted completely.
3. Stir in the spinach and water and cook for about 4-5 minutes.
4. Stir in the salt, black pepper, and lemon juice and remove from heat.
5. Serve immediately.

Nutritional Information per Serving
Calories: 298
Fat: 26.6g
Sat Fat: 16.5g
Cholesterol: 79mg

Sodium: 365mg

Carbohydrates: 9.3g

Fiber: 3.7g

Sugar: 1.9g

Protein: 8.8g

Creamy Brussels Sprouts

Brussels sprouts are mellowed by the combo of whipping cream, mustard, and garlic nicely. Surely this side dish will satisfy veggie haters too.

Yield: 5 servings

Preparation time: 15 minutes

Cooking time: 15 minutes

Allergens: dairy

Ingredients:

- 1½ pounds fresh Brussels sprouts, trimmed and halved
- 3 garlic cloves, minced
- 2 tablespoons butter, melted
- 2 tablespoons Dijon mustard
- ½ cup heavy whipping cream
- Salt and freshly ground white pepper, to taste

Instructions:

1. Preheat your oven to 450° F. (230° C)

1. In a large roasting pan, add Brussels sprouts, garlic and butter and toss to coat well.
2. Roast for about 10-15 minutes, tossing occasionally.
3. Meanwhile, in a small pan, add remaining ingredients over medium-low heat and bring to a gentle boil.
4. Cook for about 1-2 minutes, stirring continuously.
5. Serve Brussels sprouts with the topping of creamy sauce.

Nutritional Information per Serving

Calories: 146

Fat: 9.5g

Sat Fat: 5.8g

Cholesterol: 29mg

Sodium: 151mg

Carbohydrates: 13.3g

Fiber: 5.1g

Sugar: 3g

Protein: 5.1g

Cheesy Cauliflower

A really delicious baked recipe to prepare cauliflower...
Combination of mustard, mayonnaise, cheese, and butter
gives a tasty richness to cauliflower.

Yield: 4 servings

Preparation time: 10 minutes

Cooking time: 30 minutes

Allergens: dairy

Ingredients:

- 1 head cauliflower
- 1 tablespoon prepared mustard
- 1 teaspoon mayonnaise
- ¼ cup butter, cut into small pieces
- ½ cup Parmesan cheese, grated

Instructions:

1. Preheat your oven to 375° F (190° C).
2. In a bowl, add the mustard and mayonnaise and
   mix until well combined.

3. Coat the cauliflower head with the mustard mixture evenly.
4. Arrange the cauliflower head in a baking dish and top with the butter in the shape of dots, followed by the Parmesan cheese evenly.
5. Bake for about 30 minutes.
6. Remove from the oven and cut the cauliflower head into desired sized pieces and serve hot.

Nutritional Information per Serving
Calories: 162
Fat: 14.6g
Sat Fat: 8.6g
Cholesterol: 39mg
Sodium: 241mg
Carbohydrates: 4g
Fiber: 1.8g
Sugar: 1.7g
Protein: 5.6g

Stuffed Zucchini

A unique stuffed zucchini recipe for a tasty and filling lunch... These stuffed boats are the perfect way to enjoy your fresh summer zucchini.

Yield: 8 servings

Preparation time: 15 minutes

Cooking time: 18 minutes

Allergens: dairy

Ingredients:

- 4 medium zucchinis, halved lengthwise
- 1 cup red bell pepper, seeded and minced
- ½ cup Kalamata olives, pitted and minced
- ½ cup fresh tomatoes, minced
- 1 teaspoon garlic, minced
- 1 tablespoon dried oregano, crushed
- Salt and ground black pepper, as required
- ½ cup feta cheese, crumbled
- ¼ cup fresh parsley, chopped finely

Instructions:

1. Preheat your oven to 350° F (180° C). Grease a large baking sheet.
2. With a melon baller, scoop out the flesh of each zucchini half. Discard the flesh.
3. In a bowl, mix together bell pepper, olives, tomato, garlic, oregano, and black pepper.
4. Stuff each zucchini half with veggie mixture evenly.
5. Arrange zucchini halves onto the prepared baking sheet and bake for about 15 minutes.
6. Now, set the oven to broiler on high.
7. Top each zucchini half with feta cheese and broil for about 3 minutes.
8. Garnish with parsley and serve hot.

Nutritional Information per Serving

Calories: 60

Fat: 3.2g

Sat Fat: 1.6g

Cholesterol: 8mg

Sodium: 190mg

Carbohydrates: 6.4g

Fiber: 2g

Sugar: 3.2g

Protein: 3g

Creamy Zucchini Noodles

One of the healthy and delicious use of zucchini for a wonderful meal... The combo of Parmesan cheese, mayonnaise, and heavy whipping cream provide a delish creamy base to zucchini noodles.

Yield: 4 servings

Preparation time: 15 minutes

Cooking time: 10 minutes

Allergens: egg, dairy

Ingredients:

- 1¼ cups heavy whipping cream
- ¼ cup mayonnaise
- Salt and ground black pepper, as required
- 30 ounces zucchini, spiralized with blade C
- 4 organic egg yolks
- 3 ounces Parmesan cheese, grated
- 2 tablespoons fresh parsley, chopped
- 2 tablespoons butter, melted

Instructions:

1. In a pan, add the heavy cream and bring to a boil.
2. Reduce the heat to low and cook until reduced.
3. Add the mayonnaise, salt, and black pepper and cook until mixture is warm enough.
4. Add the zucchini noodles and gently, stir to combine.
5. Immediately, remove from the heat.
6. Place the zucchini noodles mixture onto 4 serving plates evenly and immediately, top with the egg yolks, followed by the parmesan and parsley.
7. Drizzle with butter and serve.

Nutritional Information per Serving
Calories: 427
Fat: 39.1g
Sat Fat: 18.5g
Cholesterol: 297mg
Sodium: 412mg
Carbohydrates: 9.7g
Fiber: 2.4g
Sugar: 3.8g
Protein: 13g

Cauliflower Crust Pizza

A foolproof crispy and tasty cauliflower crust pizza with a wonderful tasty touch... Surely everyone will love to enjoy this unique pizza.

Yield: 4 servings

Preparation time: 20 minutes

Cooking time: 42 minutes

Allergens: egg, dairy

Ingredients:

For Crust:

- 1 small head cauliflower, cut into florets
- 2 large organic eggs, beaten lightly
- ½ teaspoon dried oregano
- ½ teaspoon garlic powder
- Ground black pepper, as required

For Topping:

- ½ cup sugar-free pizza sauce
- ¾ cup mozzarella cheese, shredded
- ¼ cup black olives, pitted and sliced

- 2 tablespoons Parmesan cheese, grated

Instructions:

1. Preheat your oven to 400° F (200° C). Line a baking sheet with a lightly greased parchment paper.
2. Add the cauliflower in a food processor and pulse until rice like texture is achieved.
3. In a bowl, add the cauliflower rice, eggs, oregano, garlic powder, and black pepper and mix until well combined.
4. Place the cauliflower the mixture in the center of the prepared baking sheet and with a spatula, press into a 13-inch thin circle.
5. Bake for 40 minutes or until golden-brown.
6. Remove the baking sheet from the oven.
7. Now, set the oven to broiler on high.
8. Place the tomato sauce on top of the pizza crust and with a spatula, spread evenly and sprinkle with olives, followed by the cheeses.
9. Broil for about 1-2 minutes or until the cheese is bubbly and browned.
10. Remove from oven and with a pizza cutter, cut the pizza into equal sized triangles.
11. Serve hot.

Nutritional Information per Serving

Calories: 119

Fat: 6.6g

Sat Fat: 1.8g

Cholesterol: 98mg

Sodium: 297mg

Carbohydrates: 8.6g

Fiber: 3.4g

Sugar: 3.7g

Protein: 8.3g

Cabbage Casserole

A great way to inspire non-veggie people to indulge in eating cabbage... This recipe prepares a really delicious cheesy bake.

Yield: 3 servings

Preparation time: 15 minutes

Cooking time: 30 minutes

Allergens: dairy

Ingredients:

- ½ head cabbage
- 2 scallions, chopped
- 4 tablespoons unsalted butter
- 2 ounces cream cheese, softened
- ¼ cup Parmesan cheese, grated
- ¼ cup fresh cream
- ½ teaspoon Dijon mustard
- 2 tablespoons fresh parsley, chopped
- Salt and ground black pepper, as required

Instructions:

1. Preheat your oven to 350° F (180° C).
2. Cut cabbage head into half, lengthwise. Then cut into 4 equal sized wedges.
3. In a pan of boiling water, add cabbage wedges and cook, covered for about 5 minutes.
4. Drain well and arrange cabbage wedges into a small baking dish.
5. In a small pan, melt butter and sauté onions for about 5 minutes.
6. Add the remaining ingredients and stir to combine.
7. Remove from the heat and immediately, place the cheese mixture over cabbage wedges evenly.
8. Bake for about 20 mins.

9. Remove from the oven and let it cool for about 5 minutes before serving.
10. Cut into 3 equal sized portions and serve.

Nutritional Information per Serving
Calories: 273
Fat: 24.8g
Sat Fat: 15.4g
Cholesterol: 71mg
Sodium: 313mg
Carbohydrates: 9g
Fiber: 3.4g
Sugar: 4.5g
Protein: 6.2g

Spinach Pie

A great and rich flavored dish of spinach with the combo of cheese and cream... Spinach lover would love to enjoy this savory spinach pie.

Yield: 6 servings

Preparation time: 15 minutes

Cooking time: 37 minutes

Allergens: egg, dairy

Ingredients:

- 2 tablespoons unsalted butter, divided
- 2 tablespoons yellow onion, chopped
- 1 (16-ounce) bag frozen chopped spinach, thawed and squeezed
- 1½ cups heavy cream
- 3 organic eggs
- ½ teaspoon ground nutmeg
- Salt and ground black pepper, as required
- ½ cup Swiss cheese, shredded

Instructions:

1. Preheat your oven to 375° F (190° C). Grease a 9-inch pie dish.
2. In a large skillet, melt one tablespoon of butter over medium-high heat and sauté the onion for about 4-5 minutes.
3. Add the spinach and cook for about 2-3 minutes or until all the liquid is absorbed.
4. In a bowl add cream, eggs, nutmeg, salt, and black pepper and beat until well combined.
5. Transfer the spinach mixture in the bottom of prepared pie dish evenly.
6. Place the egg mixture over spinach mixture evenly and sprinkle with Swiss cheese evenly.
7. Top with the remaining butter in the shape of dots at many places.
8. Bake for about 25-30 minutes or until top becomes golden brown.
9. Serve hot.

Nutritional Information per Serving

Calories: 223

Fat: 20g

Sat Fat: 11.7g

Cholesterol: 141mg

Sodium: 150mg
Carbohydrates: 4.6g
Fiber: 1.8g
Sugar: 0.8g
Protein: 8.1g

Green Beans with Mushrooms

Mushrooms and green beans are sautéed with garlic and seasoning for a flavorful side dish. These ingredients complement each other nicely.

Yield: 2 servings

Preparation time: 15 minutes

Cooking time: 20 minutes

Allergens: butter, cheese

Ingredients:

- 2 tablespoons butter
- 2 tablespoons yellow onion, minced
- ½ teaspoon garlic, minced
- 1 (8-ounce) package white mushrooms, sliced
- 1 cup frozen green beans
- Salt and ground black pepper, as required
- 2 tablespoons Parmesan cheese, grated

Instructions:

1. Melt butter in a skillet over medium and sauté onion and garlic for about 1 minute.
2. Add the mushrooms and cook for about 6-7 minutes.
3. Stir in the green beans and cook for about 5-10 minutes or until desired doneness.
4. Serve hot with the garnishing of parmesan cheese.

Nutritional Information per Serving
Calories: 166
Fat: 13.1g
Sat Fat: 7.9g
Cholesterol: 35mg
Sodium: 213mg
Carbohydrates: 8.8g
Fiber: 3.2g
Sugar: 3.2g
Protein: 6.8g

Mixed Veggie Combo

An easy and quick recipe that prepares a veggie combo at its best... This wholesome fresh veggie meal is perfect for a filling lunch.

Yield: 6 servings

Preparation time: 15 minutes

Cooking time: 10 minutes

Allergens: dairy

Ingredients:

- 3 tablespoons unsalted butter
- 1 pound frozen okra, thawed, trimmed and sliced
- 1 green bell pepper, seeded and chopped
- 2 celery stalks, chopped
- 1 small yellow onion, chopped
- 2 cups tomatoes, chopped finely
- Salt and ground black pepper, as required

Instructions:

1. In a large non-stick skillet, melt butter over medium and sauté okra, bell pepper, celery, and onion for about 5-6 minutes.
2. Stir in the tomatoes, salt, and black pepper and cook for about 3-4 minutes.
3. Serve hot.

Nutritional Information per Serving

Calories: 104

Fat: 6.1g

Sat Fat: 3.7g

Cholesterol: 15mg

Sodium: 82mg

Carbohydrates: 10g

Fiber: 3.8g

Sugar: 4.3g

Protein: 2.4g

Veggie Curry

A filling and delicious aromatic mixed vegetable curry that will satisfy your tummy... Curry powder enhances the delicious flavor of all the vegetables in this baked curry.

Yield: 6 servings

Preparation time: 20 minutes

Cooking time: 20 minutes

Allergens: absent

Ingredients:

- 1 medium zucchini, chopped
- 1 medium yellow squash, chopped
- 1 green bell pepper, seeded and cubed
- 1 red bell pepper, seeded and cubed
- 1 yellow onion, sliced thinly
- 2 tablespoons olive oil
- 2 teaspoons red curry powder
- Salt and ground black pepper, as required
- ¼ cup homemade vegetable broth
- ¼ cup fresh cilantro leaves, chopped finely

Instructions:

1. Preheat your oven to 375° F (190° C). Lightly, grease a large baking dish.
2. Add all the ingredients in a bowl except the cilantro and mix until well combined.
3. Transfer the vegetable mixture into the prepared baking dish evenly.
4. Bake for about 15-20 minutes or until the desired doneness of the vegetables.
5. Serve immediately with the garnishing of cilantro.

Nutritional Information per Serving

Calories: 74

Fat: 5.1g

Sat Fat: 0.7g

Cholesterol: 0mg

Sodium: 68mg

Carbohydrates: 7.4g

Fiber: 1.9g

Sugar: 4g

Protein: 1.7g

Snack Recipes

Spiced Almonds

One of the best snacks for any season of the year... The combo of spices provides the just right amount of flavoring to the almonds.

Yield: 8 servings

Preparation time: 10 minutes

Cooking time: 10 minutes

Allergens: nuts

Ingredients:

- 2 cups whole almonds
- 1 tablespoon chili powder
- ½ teaspoon ground cinnamon
- ½ teaspoon ground cumin
- ½ teaspoon ground coriander
- Salt and ground black pepper, as required
- 1 tablespoon olive oil

Instructions:

1. Preheat your oven to 350° F (180° C). Line a baking pan with a parchment paper.
2. Add all ingredients in a bowl and toss to coat well.
3. Spread the almond mixture into the prepared baking dish in a single layer.
4. Roast for about 10 minutes, flipping twice.
5. Remove from the oven and let cool completely before serving.
6. You can preserve these roasted almonds in an airtight jar.

Nutritional Information per Serving

Calories: 156

Fat: 13.8g

Sat Fat: 1.2g

Cholesterol: 0mg

Sodium: 29mg

Carbohydrates: 5.8g

Fiber: 3.4g

Sugar: 1.1g

Protein: 5.2g

Lemony & Spicy Pumpkin Seeds

A really best way to roast fresh pumpkin seeds for a snack... Roasting gives a delicious and nice flavor to pumpkin seeds.

Yield: 4 servings

Preparation time: 10 minutes

Cooking time: 20 minutes

Allergens: absent

Ingredients:

- 1 cup pumpkin seeds, washed and dried
- 2 teaspoons garam masala
- 1/3 teaspoon red chili powder
- ¼ teaspoon ground turmeric
- Salt, to taste
- 3 tablespoons coconut oil, melted
- ½ tablespoon fresh lemon juice

Instructions:

1. Preheat your oven to 350° F (180° C). Lightly, grease a baking sheet.
2. Add all ingredients in a bowl except lemon juice and toss to coat well.
3. Transfer the pumpkin need mixture onto the prepared baking sheet.
4. Roast for about 20 minutes, flipping occasionally.
5. Remove from the oven and let cool completely before serving.
6. Drizzle with lemon juice and serve.

Nutritional Information per Serving

Calories: 274

Fat: 26.1g

Sat Fat: 11.38g

Cholesterol: 0mg

Sodium: 50mg

Carbohydrates: 6.4g

Fiber: 1.5g

Sugar: 0.4g

Protein: 8.6g

Kale Chips

Salty, crispy, addicting, and addictive kale chips from a garden to the oven in just 15 minutes... These crunchy, addictive chips will have your whole family begging for more kale chips.

Yield: 6 servings

Preparation time: 10 minutes

Cooking time: 15 minutes

Allergens: absent

Ingredients:

- 1 pound fresh kale leaves, stemmed and torn
- ¼ teaspoon cayenne pepper
- Salt, to taste
- 1 tablespoon olive oil

Instructions:

1. Preheat your oven to 350º F (180º C). Line a large baking sheet.
2. Arrange the kale pieces onto the prepared baking sheet in a single layer.
3. Sprinkle the kale with cayenne pepper and salt and drizzle with oil.
4. Bake for about 10-15 mins.
5. Remove from the oven and let it cool before serving.

Nutritional Information per Serving

Calories: 57

Fat: 2.3g

Sat Fat: 0.3g

Cholesterol: 0mg

Sodium: 60mg

Carbohydrates: 8g

Fiber: 1.2g
Sugar: 0g
Protein: 26.3g

Deviled Eggs

A great and fun twist on traditional deviled eggs... These classically delicious deviled eggs are great for family and friend's gathering.

Yield: 6 servings

Preparation time: 15 minutes

Cooking time: 5 minutes

Allergens: egg

Ingredients:

- 6 large organic eggs
- 1 medium avocado, peeled, pitted and chopped
- 2 teaspoons fresh lime juice
- Salt, to taste
- Pinch of cayenne pepper

Instructions:

1. In a large pan of water, add the eggs and bring to a boil over high heat.

2. Cover the pan and immediately remove from the heat.
3. Set aside, covered for at least 10-15 minutes.
4. Drain the eggs and let them cool completely.
5. Peel the eggs and with a sharp knife, slice them in half vertically.
6. Now, remove the yolks from egg halves.
7. In a bowl, add half of the egg yolks, avocado, lime juice, and salt and with a fork, mash until well combined.
8. Scoop the avocado mixture in the egg halves evenly.
9. Serve with the sprinkling of cayenne pepper.

Nutritional Information per Serving
Calories: 140
Fat: 11.5g
Sat Fat: 2.6g
Cholesterol: 186mg
Sodium: 99mg
Carbohydrates: 3.3g
Fiber: 2.3g
Sugar: 0.6g
Protein: 6.9g

Cheese Biscuits

One of the best cheesy biscuits with a wonderful aroma and texture… These amazing cheesy biscuits are rich in taste.

Yield: 8 servings

Preparation time: 15 minutes

Cooking time: 15 minutes

Allergens: egg, dairy

Ingredients:

- 1/3 cup coconut flour, sifted
- ¼ teaspoon organic baking powder
- Salt, to taste
- 4 organic eggs
- ¼ cup butter, melted and cooled
- 1 cup cheddar cheese, shredded

Instructions:

1. Preheat your oven to 400° F (200° C). Line a large cookie sheet with a greased piece of foil.

2. In a large bowl, add the flour, baking powder, garlic powder, and salt and mix until well combined.

3. In another bowl, add the eggs and butter and beat until smooth.

4. Add the egg mixture into the bowl of flour mixture and beat until well combined.

5. Fold in the cheddar cheese.

6. With a tablespoon, place the mixture onto prepared the cookie sheets in a single layer and with your fingers, press slightly.

7. Bake for 15 minutes or until top becomes golden brown.

8. Remove the cookie sheet from oven and place onto a wire rack to cool for about 5 minutes.

9. Carefully invert the biscuits onto the wire rack to cool completely before serving.

Nutritional Information per Serving
Calories: 142
Fat: 12.4g
Sat Fat: 7.4g
Cholesterol: 112mg
Sodium: 80mg
Carbohydrates: 0.7g
Fiber: 0.2g
Sugar: 0.3g

Protein: 6.4g

Herbed Sesame Seeds Crackers

An impressive and easy recipe of delicious homemade crackers... Fresh herbs give a wonderfully refreshing taste to these crackers.

Yield: 30 servings

Preparation time: 20 minutes

Cooking time: 40 minutes

Allergens: egg, nuts

Ingredients:

- ½ cup sesame seeds, toasted and roughly ground
- 1 cup almond flour
- ¼ cup coconut flour
- 2 tablespoons tapioca flour
- ½ teaspoon fresh thyme, chopped finely
- ½ teaspoon fresh rosemary, chopped finely
- ½ teaspoon onion powder
- ½ teaspoon garlic powder
- Salt and ground black pepper, as required
- 2 large organic eggs
- 3 tablespoons olive oil

Instructions:

1. Preheat your oven to 375° F (190° C). Line a baking sheet.
2. In a bowl, add the sesame seeds, all flours, fresh herbs and seasoning, and mix until well combined.
3. In another bowl, add the eggs and oil and beat until well combined.
4. Add the egg mixture into the flour mixture and mix until well combined.
5. Now with your hands, knead the mixture until a dough forms.
6. Arrange the dough between 2 large parchment papers and place onto a smooth surface.
7. With a rolling pin, roll the dough into 1/8-inch thickness.
8. Remove the upper parchment paper.
9. With a knife, cut the dough into 40 equal sized crackers.
10. Carefully, place the crackers onto the prepared baking sheet in a single layer.
11. Bake for 13 to 14 minutes or until golden brown.
12. Remove from the oven and let cool completely before serving.
13. You can preserve these crackers in an airtight jar.

Nutritional Information per Serving

Calories: 54

Fat: 4.8g

Sat Fat: 0.6g

Cholesterol: 12mg

Sodium: 9mg

Carbohydrates: 2g

Fiber: 0.7g

Sugar: 0.2g

Protein: 1.7g

3 Cheese Tomato Slices

A wonderful way to enjoy the garden-fresh tomatoes as a party snack... These cheesy baked tomato slices are beautiful and delicious as well.

Yield: 10 servings

Preparation time: 15 minutes

Cooking time: 15 minutes

Allergens: dairy

Ingredients:

- ½ cup mayonnaise
- ½ cup ricotta cheese, shredded
- ½ cup part-skim mozzarella cheese, shredded
- ½ cup Parmesan and Romano cheese blend, grated
- 1 teaspoon garlic, minced
- 1 tablespoon dried oregano, crushed
- Salt, to taste
- 4 large tomatoes, cut each one in 5 slices

Instructions:

1. Preheat your oven to broiler on high. Arrange a rack about 3-inch from the heating element.
2. In a bowl, add the mayonnaise, cheeses, garlic, oregano, and salt and mix until well combined and smooth.
3. Spread the cheese mixture over each tomato slice evenly.
4. Arrange the tomato slices in a broiler pan in a single layer.
5. Broil for about 3-5 minutes or until top becomes golden brown.
6. Remove from the oven and transfer the tomato slices onto a platter.
7. Set aside to cool slightly.
8. Serve warm.

Nutritional Information per Serving
Calories: 110
Fat: 57.4g
Sat Fat: 2.6g
Cholesterol: 16mg
Sodium: 227mg
Carbohydrates: 6.7g
Fiber: 1.1g
Sugar: 2.7g
Protein: 5g

Cheesy Zucchini Sticks

One of the delicious cheesy snack that is light in texture but rich in taste... Surely you would receive huge appreciation after preparing this snack.

Yield: 8 servings

Preparation time: 15 minutes

Cooking time: 25 minutes

Allergens: egg, dairy, nuts

Ingredients:

- 2 large zucchinis, cut into 3-inch sticks lengthwise
- Salt, to taste
- 2 organic eggs
- ½ cup Parmesan cheese, grated
- ½ cup almonds, finely ground
- ½ teaspoon Italian herb seasoning

Instructions:

1. In a large colander, place the zucchini sticks and sprinkle with salt.

2. Set aside for about 1 hour to drain.
3. Preheat your oven to 425° F (220° C). Line a baking sheet.
4. With your hands, squeeze the zucchini sticks to remove the excess liquid.
5. With a paper towel, pat-dry the zucchini sticks.
6. In a bowl, crack the eggs and beat well.
7. In another shallow bowl, add the remaining ingredients and mix until well combined.
8. Dip the zucchini sticks into the egg and then coat with the cheese mixture evenly.
9. Arrange the zucchini sticks onto the prepared baking sheet in a single layer.
10. Bake for 25 minutes, flipping once halfway through.

Nutritional Information per Serving
Calories: 76
Fat: 5.4g
Sat Fat: 1.2g
Cholesterol: 45mg
Sodium: 834mg
Carbohydrates: 3g
Fiber: 1.3g
Sugar: 1.2g
Protein: 5.2g

Spicy Chicken Nuggets

An awesome kid's friendly recipe that will also become an adult's favorite one too... Surely these nuggets will become a great choice for the party's snack menu.

Yield: 6 servings

Preparation time: 15 minutes

Cooking time: 10 minutes

Allergens: egg, nuts

Ingredients:

- 2 (8-ounce) grass-fed skinless, boneless chicken breasts, cut into nuggets shape
- 2 large organic eggs
- ½ cup tapioca flour
- ½ cups blanched almond flour
- ½ teaspoon paprika
- ½ teaspoon onion powder
- ½ teaspoon garlic powder
- ½ teaspoon salt
- ¼ teaspoon freshly ground black pepper
- 3-4 tablespoons olive oil

Instructions:

1. In a bowl, crack two eggs and beat well.
2. In another shallow bowl, add the flours and spices and mix until well combined.
3. Dip the chicken nuggets in beaten eggs and then coat with the flour mixture evenly.
4. Heat oil in a large skillet over medium and cook the chicken nuggets for 5 minutes per side or until golden brown.
5. Remove from the heat and transfer the nuggets onto a platter.
6. Set aside to cool slightly.
7. Serve warm.

Nutritional Information per Serving

Calories: 270

Fat: 15.8g

Sat Fat: 2.9g

Cholesterol: 106mg

Sodium: 248mg

Carbohydrates: 11g

Fiber: 1.1g

Sugar: 0.3g

Protein: 21.1g

Cheesy Tilapia Strips

Really delicious, healthy and nutritious snack recipe for all... These delicious tilapia fish sticks are moist from inside and crunchy from outside.

Yield: 6 servings

Preparation time: 15 minutes

Cooking time: 20 minutes

Allergens: egg, dairy, nuts

Ingredients:

- 1 pound tilapia fillets, cut into strips
- 1 cup almond flour
- Salt and ground black pepper, as required
- 2 large organic eggs, beaten
- 1½ cups Parmesan cheese, shredded

Instructions:

1. Preheat your oven to 450° F (230° C) and line a baking sheet.

2. In a shallow bowl, add the flour, salt, and black pepper and mix until well combined.
3. In a second shallow bowl, place the eggs and a splash of water and beat well.
4. In a third shallow bowl, place the cheese.
5. Coat the tilapia strips with the flour mixture, then dip into the beaten eggs and finally, coat with the cheese.
6. Arrange the tilapia strips onto the prepared baking sheet in a single layer.
7. Bake for about 18-20 minutes or until done completely.
8. Remove from the heat and transfer the tilapia strips onto a platter.
9. Set aside to cool slightly.
10. Serve warm.

Nutritional Information per Serving
Calories: 281
Fat: 16.7g
Sat Fat: 5g
Cholesterol: 113mg
Sodium: 423mg
Carbohydrates: 4.8g
Fiber: 2g
Sugar: 0.1g

Protein: 27.7g

Spicy Tuna Croquettes

One of the healthy and fancy looking snacks for family and friend's gathering... These tuna croquettes are spicy and incredibly flavorful.

Yield: 8 servings

Preparation time: 20 minutes

Cooking time: 20 minutes

Allergens: egg, nuts

Ingredients:

- 2 (5-ounce) cans tuna, drained
- 1 tablespoon coconut oil
- ½ of large yellow onion, chopped
- 1 (1-inch) piece fresh ginger, minced
- 3 small garlic cloves, minced
- 1 medium Serrano pepper, seeded and minced
- ½ teaspoon ground coriander
- ¼ teaspoon ground turmeric
- ¼ teaspoon red chili powder
- ¼ teaspoon garam masala
- Salt and ground black pepper, as required

- 1 cup cooked sweet potato, peeled and mashed
- 1 organic egg
- ¼ cup tapioca flour
- ¼ cup almond flour
- ½ cup olive oil

Instructions:

1. Melt coconut oil in a frying pan over medium heat and sauté the onion, ginger, garlic and Serrano pepper for about 5-6 minutes.
2. Stir in the spices and sauté for about 1 minute more.
3. Remove from heat and place the onion mixture into a bowl.
4. Add the tuna and sweet potato and mix until well combined.
5. Make equal sized oblong shaped patties from the mixture.
6. Arrange the croquettes onto a baking sheet in a single layer and refrigerate overnight.
7. In a shallow bowl, crack the egg and beat well.
8. In another shallow bowl, add the flours and mix well.

9. Heat oil in a large skillet and add the croquettes in 2 batches and shallow fry for about 2-3 minutes per side.
10. With a slotted spoon, transfer the croquettes onto a paper towel-lined plate to drain completely.
11. Serve warm.

Nutritional Information per Serving

Calories: 259

Fat: 19.6g

Sat Fat: 4.8g

Cholesterol: 31mg

Sodium: 55mg

Carbohydrates: 10g

Fiber: 1.5g

Sugar: 2.2g

Protein: 11.6g

Drink Recipes

Hot Chocolate

One of the quick and easy to prepare hot chocolate recipes... This hot chocolate is prepared with only five simple ingredients.

Yield: 2 servings

Preparation time: 10 minutes

Allergens: dairy

Ingredients:

- 2 ounces unsalted butter
- 4 tablespoons cacao powder

- 2 teaspoons powdered Erythritol
- ½ teaspoon organic vanilla extract
- 2 cups boiling water
- 2 tablespoons whipped cream

Instructions:

1. In a tall beaker, place all the ingredients and with an immersion blender, blend for about 15-20 seconds or until a fine foam appears on top.
2. Transfer the hot chocolate into 2 mugs.
3. Top each mug with whipped cream and serve.

Nutritional Information per Serving

Calories: 269

Fat: 29.1g

Sat Fat: 18.4g

Cholesterol: 78mg

Sodium: 169mg

Carbohydrates: 4.3g

Fiber: 2.3g

Sugar: 0.2g

Protein: 2.1g

Chai Spiced Hot Chocolate

An aromatic hot chocolate that has the flavor of cacao powder with a hint of spices... Surely this recipe will take your hot chocolate to the next level.

Yield: 2 servings

Preparation time: 10 minutes

Cooking time: 5 minutes

Allergens: nuts

Ingredients:

- 2 chai tea bags
- ½ cup hot water, divided
- 4 tablespoons cacao powder
- 1 cup unsweetened almond milk
- ½ teaspoon stevia powder
- 4 tablespoons cacao butter

Instructions:

1. In a bowl, add tea bag and 2 tablespoons of water.
2. Let it steep for about 5 minutes.

3. In a small pan, add cacao powder and remaining water and beat well.
4. Add the almond milk and stir to combine.
5. Stir in stevia and cacao butter.
6. Discard the tea bag from the cup and pour the tea into the pan.
7. Cook for about 2-4 minutes or until butter is dissolved completely, stirring continuously.
8. Remove from the heat and transfer into serving cups.
9. Serve immediately.

Nutritional Information per Serving
Calories: 161
Fat: 17.3g
Sat Fat: 9.1g
Cholesterol: 0mg
Sodium: 90mg
Carbohydrates: 6g
Fiber: 3.5g
Sugar: 0g
Protein: 2.5g

Butter Coffee

An amazing way to enjoy coffee with deliciousness...This butter coffee will energize you with great health benefits.

Yield: 2 servings

Preparation time: 5 minutes

Cooking time: 5 minutes

Allergens: dairy

Ingredients:

- 2 cups water
- 2 tablespoons ground coffee
- 1 tablespoon coconut oil
- 1 tablespoon butter

Instructions:

1. In a pan, add the water and coffee over medium heat and cook for about 5 minutes.
2. Through a strainer, strain the coffee into a blender.
3. Add the coconut oil and butter and pulse until light and creamy.
4. Transfer into 2 mugs and serve immediately.

Nutritional Information per Serving

Calories: 110

Fat: 12.6g

Sat Fat: 9.5g

Cholesterol: 15mg

Sodium: 48mg

Carbohydrates: 0g

Fiber: 0g

Sugar: 0g

Protein: 0.1g

Gingerbread Latte

One of the perfect cozy homemade drink for winter season... This gingerbread latte recipe is definitely delicious.

Yield: 2 servings

Preparation time: 10 minutes

Allergens: nuts

Ingredients:

- ½ cup strong brewed coffee
- 2 tablespoons yacon syrup
- ½ teaspoon ground cinnamon
- ½ teaspoon ground ginger
- ¼ teaspoon ground nutmeg
- ½ teaspoon vanilla extract
- 1¾ cups hot unsweetened almond milk

Instructions:

1. Place all ingredients in a bowl except the almond milk and beat until well combined.
2. Place the coffee mixture into 2 coffee mugs evenly and top with the milk.
3. Spoon foam over the top and serve.

Nutritional Information per Serving
Calories: 68
Fat: 3.2g
Sat Fat: 0.3g
Cholesterol: 0mg
Sodium: 166mg
Carbohydrates: 8.8g
Fiber: 1.3g
Sugar: 3.7g
Protein: 1g

Espresso Coffee

A rich, creamy and frothy coffee that can be prepared at home easily... Surely everyone would love to enjoy this frothy coffee.

Yield: 2 servings

Preparation time: 10 minutes

Allergens: nuts

Ingredients:

- 3-4tablespoons Erythritol
- 2 tablespoons instant coffee powder

- 2 teaspoons water
- 2 cups hot almond milk

Instructions:

1. In 2 coffee mugs, divide the Erythritol, coffee powder and water and stir until well combined.
2. With a spoon, beat vigorously until frothy.
3. Pour hot milk over the whipped coffee paste in each mug and stir to combine.
4. Serve immediately.

Nutritional Information per Serving

Calories: 40

Fat: 3.5g

Sat Fat: 0.3g

Cholesterol: 0mg

Sodium: 180mg

Carbohydrates: 2g

Fiber: 1g

Sugar: 0g

Protein: 1g

Spiced Tea

A wonderfully delicious hot tea with an aromatic touch of whole warm spices... The combo of warm spices infuses the black tea very nicely.

Yield: 2 servings

Preparation time: 10 minutes

Cooking time: 5 minutes

Allergens: nuts

Ingredients:

- 1 cup water
- 2 whole cloves
- 2 green cardamom pods
- Pinch of fennel seeds
- 2 black tea bags
- 1 cup unsweetened almond milk
- 12-14 drops liquid stevia

Instructions:

1. In a small pan, add the water and spices over medium-low heat and bring to a gentle simmer

2. Add the tea bags and immediately, cover the pan for about 2 minutes.
3. Add the almond milk and bring to a boil.
4. Immediately, remove from the heat and set aside covered for at least 1 minute.
5. Through a fine mesh strainer, strain the tea into serving cups.
6. Stir in the stevia and serve immediately.

Nutritional Information per Serving
Calories: 21
Fat: 1.8g
Sat Fat: 0.2g
Cholesterol: 0mg
Sodium: 90mg
Carbohydrates: 1.2g
Fiber: 0g
Sugar: 0g
Protein: 0.5g

Ginger Tea

A best and healthy drink that is great for digestion and is soothing and healing as well... This piping hot cup of ginger tea will beat the cold in the winter nicely.

Yield: 4 servings

Preparation time: 10 minutes

Cooking time: 15 minutes

Allergens: absent

Ingredients:

- 6 cups water
- ½ of lemon, seeded and chopped roughly
- 1 (1-inch) piece fresh ginger, peeled and chopped
- 2 tablespoons yacon syrup
- Pinch of ground turmeric
- Pinch of ground cinnamon

Instructions:

1. In a pan, add all ingredients over medium-high heat and bring to a boil.

2. Reduce the heat to medium and cook for about 10-12 minutes.
3. Remove from the heat and through a strainer, strain the tea into serving cups.
4. Serve hot.

Nutritional Information per Serving
Calories: 15
Fat: 0.1g
Sat Fat: 0g
Cholesterol: 0mg
Sodium: 3mg
Carbohydrates: 3.6g
Fiber: 0.2g
Sugar: 1.8g
Protein: 0.1g

Eggnog

One of the best recipe of homemade eggnog... This homemade eggnog is thick and creamy and full of perfect flavoring alongside the taste of cinnamon and nutmeg.

Yield: 6 servings

Preparation time: 15 minutes

Cooking time: 15 minutes

Allergens: egg, dairy, nuts

Ingredients:

- 4 large organic eggs, whites and yolks separated
  2 cups heavy whipping cream
- 1 cup unsweetened almond milk
- ¾ cup powdered Erythritol
- ½ teaspoon organic vanilla extract
- ¼ teaspoon ground cinnamon
- ¼ teaspoon ground nutmeg

Instructions:

1. In a bowl, add the egg yolks and beat until smooth.
2. In a pan, add the heavy cream, almond milk, Erythritol and beaten egg yolks over medium-low heat and cook for about 10-15 minutes, stirring continuously.
3. Remove from the heat and transfer the mixture into a heatproof bowl.
4. Add the vanilla extract and spices and beat until well combined.
5. Set aside to cool completely.
6. Cover the bowl and refrigerate overnight.
7. Remove from the refrigerator and through a strainer, strain the mixture.
8. Transfer the eggnog into serving glasses and serve.

Nutritional Information per Serving

Calories: 56

Fat: 3.9g

Sat Fat: 1.1g

Cholesterol: 124mg

Sodium: 77mg

Carbohydrates: 0.8g

Fiber: 0.2g

Sugar: 0.3g

Protein: 4.4g

Mint Green Tea

A refreshingly delicious cold tea that is good for everyone... Fresh mint leaves and green tea create this tea an ideal summer standout.

Yield: 4 servings

Preparation time: 10 minutes

Allergens: absent

Ingredients:

- 2½ cups boiling water
- 1 cup fresh mint leaves
- 4 green tea bags
- 2 teaspoons yacon syrup

Instructions:

1. In a pitcher, add the water, mint and tea bags and mix until well combined.
2. Cover and steep for about 5 minutes.
3. Refrigerate for at least 3 hours.
4. Discard the tea bags and divide the tea into serving glasses.

5. Add the yacon syrup and stir to combine.
6. Serve.

Nutritional Information per Serving

Calories: 14

Fat: 0.2g

Sat Fat: 0g

Cholesterol: 0mg

Sodium: 8mg

Carbohydrates: 2.9g

Fiber: 1.6g

Sugar: 0.6g

Protein: 0.8g

Iced Coffee

One of the easiest and well blended iced coffee recipe...
This recipe will help you to make your favorite iced coffees
at home easily.

Yield: 2 servings

Preparation time: 10 minutes

Allergens: dairy

Ingredients:

- 2 cups chilled coffee
- 2 tablespoons heavy cream
- 1 tablespoon MCT oil
- 1 cup ice cubes plus more
- 1 teaspoon organic vanilla extract
- ½ teaspoon liquid stevia
- ¼ teaspoon xanthan gum
- ¼ teaspoon ground cinnamon
- Pinch of sea salt

Instructions:

1. In a blender, add the coffee, heavy cream, MCT oil and 1 cup of ice cubes and pulse on high speed until well combined.
2. Add the remaining ingredients and pulse until smooth.
3. Add the desired amount of ice cubes into glasses.
4. Pour coffee over ice and serve.

Nutritional Information per Serving

Calories: 118

Fat: 12.6g

Sat Fat: 10.5g

Cholesterol: 21mg

Sodium: 163mg

Carbohydrates: 2.6g

Fiber: 1.8g

Sugar: 0.3g

Protein: 0.6g

Ginger Lemonade

A wonderfully delicious twist on traditional lemonade...
This refreshing lemonade will be an ultimate summer
delight for all family members.

Yield: 4 servings

Preparation time: 10 minutes

Allergens: absent

Ingredients:

- 2 lemons, juiced
- 2 tablespoons fresh ginger, peeled and grated
- 1/3 cup powdered Erythritol
- 4 cups water
- 1ce cubes, as required

Instructions:

1. In a pitcher, add the lemon juice, ginger, and
   Erythritol and water and stir until sweetener is
   dissolved.
2. Fill 4 serving glasses with ice and top with the
   lemonade.

3. Serve chilled.

Nutritional Information per Serving

Calories: 13

Fat: 0.3g

Sat Fat: 0.2g

Cholesterol: 0mg

Sodium: 11mg

Carbohydrates: 2.2g

Fiber: 0.4g

Sugar: 0.4g

Protein: 0.4g

Dessert Recipes

Mocha Ice Cream

A decadent homemade ice-cream... This homemade ice cream gets its rich flavor from coffee and cacao powder.

Yield: 2 servings

Preparation time: 15 minutes

Allergens: dairy

Ingredients:

- 1 cup unsweetened coconut milk
- ¼ cup heavy cream

- 2 tablespoons Erythritol
- 15 drops liquid stevia
- 2 tablespoons cacao powder
- 1 tablespoon instant coffee
- ¼ teaspoon xanthan gum

Instructions:

1. In a container, add all the ingredients except xanthan gum and with an immersion blender, blend until well combined.
2. Slowly, add the xanthan gum and blend until a slightly thicker mixture is formed.
3. Transfer the mixture into ice cream maker and process according to manufacturer's instructions.
4. Now, transfer the ice cream into an airtight container and freeze for at least 4-5 hours before serving.

Nutritional Information per Serving
Calories: 339
Fat: 35.2g
Sat Fat: 29.5g
Cholesterol: 21mg
Sodium: 33mg
Carbohydrates: 10g

Fiber: 4.6g

Sugar: 4g

Protein: 4.1g

Frozen Avocado Yogurt

A sweet and creamy frozen yogurt with prettiest pale green color...This summer frozen treat is a surprisingly delicious

Yield: 3 servings

Preparation time: 15 minutes

Allergens: dairy, nuts

Ingredients:

- 2 medium avocados, peeled, pitted and chopped
- ½ cup unsweetened almond milk
- ½ cup plain Greek yogurt
- 1 teaspoon liquid stevia
- 2 tablespoons fresh lemon juice
- 1 teaspoon organic vanilla extract
- 1 teaspoon fresh mint leaves

Instructions:

1. In a blender, add all ingredients except for mint leaves and pulse until creamy and smooth.

2. Transfer into an airtight container and freeze for at least 2-3 hours.

3. Remove from the freezer and set aside for at least 10-15 minutes.

4. With a wooden spoon, stir well and serve with a topping of fresh mint leaves.

Nutritional Information per Serving

Calories: 235

Fat: 18.8g

Sat Fat: 3g

Cholesterol: 2mg

Sodium: 70mg

Carbohydrates: 12g

Fiber: 8g

Sugar: 3.6g

Protein: 4.9g

Lemon Mousse

A refreshing and satisfying sweet treat for the whole family... This recipe will be perfect for a quick dessert.

Yield: 4 servings

Preparation time: 10 minutes

Allergens: dairy

Ingredients:

- ¼ cup fresh lemon juice
- 8 ounces cream cheese, softened
- 1 cup heavy cream
- 1/8 teaspoon salt
- ½-1 teaspoon lemon liquid stevia

Instructions:

1. In a blender, add lemon juice and cream cheese and pulse till smooth. Add remaining ingredients and pulse until well combined and fluffy.
2. Transfer the mixture into serving glasses and refrigerate to chill before serving.

Nutritional Information per Serving

Calories: 305

Fat: 31.5g

Sat Fat: 19.2g

Cholesterol: 103mg

Sodium: 206mg

Carbohydrates: 2.7g

Fiber: 0.1g

Sugar: 0.5g

Protein: 5g

Vanilla Crème Brûlée

A delicious and classic dessert for special dinner parties...
The caramelized topping is the main secret of this delicious
crème Brûlée.

Yield: 4 servings

Preparation time: 20 minutes

Cooking time: 1 hour

Allergens: egg, dairy

Ingredients:

- 2 cups heavy cream
- 1 vanilla bean, halved and scraped out seeds
- 4 organic egg yolks
- 1/3 teaspoon stevia powder
- 1 teaspoon organic vanilla extract
- Pinch of salt
- 4 tablespoon granulated Erythritol

Instructions:

1. Preheat your oven to 350° F (180° C).
2. In a pan, add the heavy cream over medium heat and cook until heated.
3. Stir in the vanilla bean seeds and bring to a gentle boil.
4. Reduce the heat to very-low and cook, covered for about 20 minutes.
5. Meanwhile, in a bowl, add the remaining ingredients except for Erythritol and beat until thick and pale mixture forms.
6. Remove the heavy cream from heat and through a fine mesh strainer, strain into a heatproof bowl.
7. Slowly, add the cream in egg yolk mixture beating continuously until well combined.
8. Divide the mixture into 4 ramekins evenly.

9. Arrange the ramekins into a large baking dish.

10. In the baking dish, add hot water about half way of the ramekins.

11. Bake for about 30-35 min.

12. Remove from the oven and let it completely cool slightly.

13. Refrigerate the ramekins for at least 4 hours.

14. Just before serving, sprinkle the ramekins with Erythritol evenly.

15. Holding a kitchen torch about 4-5-inches from the top, caramelize the Erythritol for about 2 minutes.

16. Set aside for 5 minutes before serving.

Nutritional Information per Serving

Calories: 264

Fat: 26.7

Sat Fat: 19.4g

Cholesterol: 292mg

Sodium: 31mg

Carbohydrates: 2.4g

Fiber: 0g

Sugar: 0.3g

Protein: 3.9g

Cream Cheese Flan

One of the classic and super delicious recipes of flan...
Cream cheese, cream, and eggs complement each other
greatly.

Yield: 8 servings

Preparation time: 15 minutes

Cooking time: 1 hour 5 minutes

Allergens: egg, dairy

Ingredients:

- ¾ cup granulated Erythritol, divided
- 3 tablespoons water, divided
- 2 teaspoons organic vanilla extract, divided
- 5 large organic eggs
- 2 cups heavy whipping cream
- 8 ounces full-fat cream cheese, softened
- ¼ teaspoon sea salt

Instructions:

1. Preheat your oven to 350° F (180° C). Grease an 8-inch cake pan.
2. For caramel: in a heavy-bottomed pan, add ½ cup of the Erythritol, 2 tablespoons of water and 1 teaspoon of vanilla extract over medium-low heat and cook until sweetener is melted completely, stirring continuously.
3. Remove from the heat and place the caramel in the bottom of the prepared cake pan evenly.
4. In a blender, add the remaining Erythritol, vanilla extract, heavy cream, cream cheese, eggs, and salt and pulse until smooth.
5. Place the cream cheese mixture over caramel evenly.
6. Arrange the cake pan into a large roasting pan.
7. In the roasting pan, add the hot water about 1-inch up sides of the cake pan.
8. Place the roasting pan in oven and bake for about 1 hour or until center becomes set.
9. Remove from the oven and place the cake pan in the water bath to cool completely.
10. Refrigerate for about 4-5 hours before serving.

Nutritional Information per Serving
Calories: 250
Fat: 24.1g

Sat Fat: 14.1g

Cholesterol: 189mg

Sodium: 198mg

Carbohydrates: 2g

Fiber: 0g

Sugar: 0.5g

Protein: 6.7g

Pumpkin Custard

A luscious and richly flavored baked custard recipe for holiday dessert table... Pumpkin pie spice and liquid cinnamon stevia give a delish flavoring to pumpkin puree.

Yield: 6 servings

Preparation time: 15 minutes

Cooking time: 50 minutes

Allergens: egg, dairy

Ingredients:

- 15 ounces homemade pumpkin puree
- 4 organic eggs, beaten
- ½ cup heavy cream
- 2 teaspoons organic vanilla extract
- 1 teaspoon cinnamon liquid stevia
- 2 teaspoons pumpkin pie spice
- ¼ teaspoon salt
- 3 tablespoons whipped cream

Instructions:

1. Preheat your oven to 350° F (180° C). Lightly, grease 6 ramekins.
2. In a large bowl, add all ingredients and beat until well combined and smooth.
3. Divide the mixture into the prepared ramekins evenly.
4. Bake for 45-50 minutes or until a wooden skewer inserted in the center comes out clean.
5. Remove from the oven and let it completely cool slightly.
6. Serve warm with the topping of whipped cream.

Nutritional Information per Serving
Calories: 102
Fat: 9.8g
Sat Fat: 4.2g
Cholesterol: 131mg
Sodium: 148mg
Carbohydrates: 7g
Fiber: 2.1g
Sugar: 2.8g
Protein: 4.9g

No-Bake Strawberry Cheesecake

An incredibly luscious and yummy dessert of cheesecake...
This light and fluffy no-bake cheesecake is packed with the
flavor of fresh strawberries.

Yield: 8 servings

Preparation time: 20 minutes

Allergens: dairy

Ingredients:

For Crust:

- ¾ cup unsweetened coconut, shredded
- ¾ cup raw sunflower seeds
- ¼ cup Erythritol
- ¼ teaspoon salt
- 3 tablespoons unsalted butter, melted

For Filling:

- 2 cups fresh strawberries, hulled and sliced
- 1½ teaspoons fresh lemon juice
- 1 teaspoon liquid stevia
- ¼ teaspoon salt

- 8 ounces cream cheese, softened
- ½ teaspoon organic vanilla extract
- 1 cup heavy cream

Instructions:

1. For crust: in a food processor, add the coconut, sunflower seeds, Erythritol and salt, and pulse until a fine crumb like the mixture is formed.
2. While motor is running, add the butter and pulse until well combined.
3. Transfer the mixture to a 9-inch pie dish and with your hands, press the mixture in the bottom and up sides of pie dish.
4. With a paper towel wipe out the blender.
5. Now, in the blender, add the strawberries, lemon juice, stevia, and salt and pulse until a puree forms.
6. Transfer the strawberry puree into a bowl.
7. In another bowl, add the cream cheese and beat until smooth.
8. Add the vanilla stevia and heavy cream and beat until fluffy.
9. Add the strawberry puree mixture and mix until well combined.
10. Place the strawberry mixture over the crust mixture evenly and freeze for at least 4-8 hours.

11. Remove from the freezer and set aside for about 5 minutes.
12. Cut into 8 equal sized slices and serve.

Nutritional Information per Serving

Calories: 254

Fat: 24.6g

Sat Fat: 14.8g

Cholesterol: 63mg

Sodium: 196mg

Carbohydrates: 6g

Fiber: 1.8g

Sugar: 2.5g

Protein: 3.9g

Creamy Matcha Cake Roll

A beautiful colored and lavish treat with a soft and smooth texture... This beautifully colored cake roll will be great for special occasions.

Yield: 10 servings

Preparation time: 20 minutes

Cooking time: 11 minutes

Allergens: egg, dairy, nuts

Ingredients:

For Cake:

- 1 cup almond flour
- ½ cup powdered Swerve
- ¼ cup matcha powder
- ¼ cup psyllium husk powder
- 1 teaspoon organic baking powder
- ½ teaspoon salt
- 3 large organic eggs
- ½ cup heavy whipping cream
- 4 tablespoons butter, melted
- 1 teaspoon organic vanilla extract

For Filling:

- 3-4 tablespoons water
- 1 packet unflavored gelatin
- 2 cups heavy whipping cream
- 2 teaspoons organic vanilla extract
- ¼ cup powdered Swerve

Instructions:

1. Preheat your oven to 350° F (180° C). Line a baking sheet.
2. For cake: in a bowl, add the almond flour, Swerve, matcha powder, psyllium husk, baking powder, and salt and mix until well combined.
3. Now, sift the flour mixture into a second bowl.
4. In a third bowl, add the remaining ingredients and beat until well combined.
5. Add the egg mixture into the bowl of flour mixture and mix until a very thick dough forms.
6. Place the dough onto the prepared baking sheet and roll into an even rectangle.
7. Bake for about 10 minutes.
8. Remove from the oven and place the baking sheet onto a wire rack to cool for about 4-5 minutes.
9. Gently, roll the warm cake with the help of parchment paper and set aside to cool completely.

10. Meanwhile, for filling: in a microwave-safe bowl, add the water and sprinkle with the gelatin.
11. Set aside for about 5 minutes.
12. Now, microwave for about 15-20 seconds.
13. Remove from the microwave and with a wire whisk, beat the gelatin mixture until smooth.
14. In the bowl of a stand mixer, add the gelatin mixture and remaining ingredients and beat until cream becomes stiff.
15. Spread the whipped cream over cooled cake evenly.
16. Carefully and gently, roll the cake and freezer for about 10 minutes before slicing.
17. With a sharp knife, cut the cake roll into desired sized slices and serve.

Nutritional Information per Serving

Calories: 246

Fat: 22.8g

Sat Fat: 10.7g

Cholesterol: 109mg

Sodium: 183mg

Carbohydrates: 6.8g

Fiber: 4g

Sugar: 0.6g

Protein: 5.6g

Chocolate Lava Cake

A spectacular cake that will be a great treat for your chocolate lover toddlers... Surely you'll make this cake over and over again.

Yield: 2 servings

Preparation time: 15 minutes

Cooking time: 9 minutes

Allergens: egg, dairy

Ingredients:

- 2 ounces 70% dark chocolate
- 2 ounces unsalted butter
- 2 organic eggs
- 2 tablespoons powdered Erythritol plus more for dusting
- 1 tablespoon almond flour
- 6 fresh raspberries

Instructions:

1. Preheat your oven to 350° F (180° C). Grease 2 ramekins.
2. In a microwave-safe bowl, add the chocolate and butter and microwave on High for about 2 minutes or until melted, stirring after every 30 seconds.
3. Remove from microwave and mix until smooth.
4. Place the eggs in a bowl and with a wire whisk, beat well.
5. Add the chocolate mixture, Erythritol, and almond flour and stir until well combined.
6. Divide the mixture into the prepared ramekins evenly.
7. Bake for about 9 minutes or until the top is set.
8. Remove from oven and set aside for about 1-2 minutes.

9. Carefully, invert the cakes onto the serving plates and dust with extra powdered Erythritol.
10. Serve with a garnishing of the strawberries.

Nutritional Information per Serving

Calories: 436

Fat: 44g

Sat Fat: 25.2g

Cholesterol: 225mg

Sodium: 232mg

Carbohydrates: 11g

Fiber: 6.1g

Sugar: 1.4g

Protein: 10.4g

Key Lime Pie

Prepare a delightfully great and refreshing dessert for your family... Surely you will receive huge appreciation from all.

Yield: 8 servings

Preparation time: 20 minutes

Cooking time: 20 minutes

Allergens: egg, dairy, nuts

Ingredients:

For Crust:

- ½cup almond flour
- ½cup coconut flour, sifted
- ¼cup granulated Erythritol
- ¼cup unsalted butter, melted
- 2 organic eggs
- ¼teaspoon salt

For Filling:

- ¾cup unsweetened coconut milk
- ½cup granulated Erythritol
- ¼cup heavy cream

- 2 teaspoons xanthan gum
- 1 teaspoon guar gum
- ¼ teaspoon powdered stevia
- 3 organic egg yolks
- ½ cup fresh key lime juice
- 2 tablespoons unsweetened dried coconut

For Topping:

- 1 cup whipped cream
- ½ key lime, cut into slices

Instructions:

1. Preheat your oven to 400° F (200° C).
2. For crust: Add all ingredients in a bowl and mix until well combined.
3. With your hands, knead the dough for about 1 minute.
4. Make a ball from the dough.
5. Arrange the dough ball between 2 sheets of wax paper and with a rolling pin, roll into a 1/8-inch thick circle.
6. In a 9-inch pie dish, place the dough and with your hands, press the mixture in the bottom and up sides.

7. Now, with a fork, prick the bottom and sides of crust at many places.

8. Bake for about 10 minutes.

9. Remove from the oven and place the crust onto a wire rack to cool.

10. Now, set the temperature of the oven to 350° F (180° C).

11. For filling: in a food processor, add the coconut milk, Erythritol, heavy cream, xanthan gum, guar gum, and stevia and pulse until well combined.

12. Add the egg yolks and lime juice and pulse until well combined.

13. Place the filling mixture over the crust and with the back of a spoon, spread evenly.

14. Bake for about 10 minutes.

15. Remove from the oven and place the pie dish onto a wire rack to cool for about 10 minutes.

16. Now, freeze the pie for about 3-4 hours before serving.

17. Remove from the freezer and garnish the pie with the whipped cream and lemon slices.

18. Cut into desired sized slices and serve.

Nutritional Information per Serving

Calories: 251

Fat: 24g

Sat Fat: 13.9g

Cholesterol: 157mg

Sodium: 162mg

Carbohydrates: 5.8g

Fiber: 3g

Sugar: 1.3g

Protein: 5.1g

Chocolaty Mascarpone Cheese Brownies

Do you like brownies that should be rich, dense, fudgy and a little bit chewy? Then, discover this secret of the perfect brownie in this easy recipe.

Yield: 16 servings

Preparation time: 20 minutes

Cooking time: 28 minutes

Allergens: egg, dairy

Ingredients:

- 5 ounces 70% dark chocolate, chopped roughly
- 4 tablespoons unsalted butter
- 3 large organic eggs
- ½ cup Erythritol
- ¼ cup mascarpone cheese
- ¼ cup cacao powder, divided
- ½ teaspoon salt

Instructions:

1. Preheat your oven to 375° F (190° C). Line a 9x9-inch baking sheet with a parchment paper.

2. In a medium microwave-safe bowl, add the chocolate and microwave on High for about 2 minutes or until melted completely, stirring after every 30 seconds.
3. Add the butter and microwave for about 1 minute or until melted and smooth, stirring once after every 10 seconds.
4. Remove from the microwave and mix until smooth.
5. Set aside to cool slightly.
6. In a large bowl, add the eggs and Erythritol and with an electric mixer, beat on high speed until frothy.
7. Add the mascarpone cheese and beat until smooth.
8. Add 2 tablespoons of the cacao powder and salt and gently stir to combine.
9. Now, sift in the remaining cacao powder and stir until well combined.
10. Pour the melted chocolate mixture into the egg mixture and mix well until well combined.
11. Place the mixture into the prepared pan evenly.
12. Bake for about 25 mins.
13. Remove from the oven and let it cool completely before cutting.
14. With a sharp knife, cut into desired sized squares and serve.

Nutritional Information per Serving

Calories: 93

Fat: 9.2g

Sat Fat: 5.5g

Cholesterol: 45mg

Sodium: 113mg

Carbohydrates: 3.5g

Fiber: 1.9g

Sugar: 0.2g

Protein: 3g

Conversion Tables

Temperature Conversion Table

Description	American Standard	Metric	Gas mark
cool	275 F	140 C	mark # 1
Luke warm cool	250 F	130 C	mark # ½
very cool	225 F	110 C	mark # ¼
cool moderate	300 F	150 C	mark # 2
very moderate	325 F	170 C	mark # 3
moderate	350 F	180 C	mark # 4
moderately hot	375 F	190 C	mark # 5
fairly hot	400 F	200 C	mark # 6
hot	425 F	220 C	mark # 7
really hot	450 F	230 C	mark # 8

very hot	475 F	240 C	mark # 9

Low Carb Sweetener Conversion Table

Sugar	1 Tsp	1 Tbsp.	1/4 Cup	1/3 Cup	1/2 Cup	1 Cup
Erythritol	1 1/4 tsp	1 Tbsp. + 1 tsp	1/3 cup	1/3 cup + 2 Tbsp.	2/3 cup	1 1/3 cup
Xylitol	1 tsp	1 Tbsp.	1/4 cup	1/3 cup	1/2 cup	1 cup
Swerve	1 tsp	1 Tbsp.	1/4 cup	1/3 cup	1/2 cup	1 cup
NuNaturals NuStevia Stevia Extract	-	-	3/16 tsp	1/4 tsp	3/8 tsp	3/4 tsp
NuNaturals NuStevia Liquid Stevia	3/8 tsp	3/8 tsp	1 1/2 tsp	2 tsp	3 tsp	2 Tbsp.
Sweet Leaf Sweet Drops Liquid Stevia	-	1/8 tsp	1/2 tsp	2/3 tsp	1 tsp	2 tsp
Sukrin:1	1 tsp	1 Tbsp.	1/4 cup	1/3 cup	1/2 cup	1 cup
THM Sweet Blend	-	1/2 tsp	2 tsp	1 Tbsp.	1 Tbsp. +2 tsp	3 Tbsp.
THM	1/3	1 tsp	1	2	3	6

Gentle Sweet	tsp		Tbsp. + 1 tsp	Tbsp.	Tbsp. + 1 tsp	Tbsp.
Truvia Spoonable	1/2 tsp	1 1/4 tsp	1 Tbsp. + 2 tsp	2 Tbsp. + 1 tsp	3 1/2 Tbsp.	1/3 + 1 1/2 Tbsp.
Pyure All-Purpose Blend	1/2 tsp	1 1/2 tsp	2 Tbsp.	2 Tbsp. + 2 tsp	1/4 cup	1/2 cup
Natural Mate All-Purpose Blend	3/8 tsp	1 1/8 tsp	1 Tbsp. + 1 1/2 tsp	2 Tbsp.	3 Tbsp.	6 Tbsp.
Pure Monk	-	-	1/6 tsp	1/4 tsp	1/3 tsp	2/3 tsp
Swanson Purelo Lo Han Sweetener	-	1/4 tsp	3/4 tsp	1 tsp	1/12 tsp	3 tsp
LakantoMonkfruit Sweetener	1 tsp	1 Tbsp.	1/4 cup	1/3 cup	1/2 cup	1 cup
MonkSweet Plus	1/2 tsp	1 1/2 tsp	2 Tbsp.	2 Tbsp. + 2 tsp	1/4 cup	1/2 cup
Just Like Sugar Table Top	1 tsp	1 Tbsp.	1/4 cup	1/3 cup	1/2 cup	1 cup

Yogurt Conversion Table

US Cups	Amount in Grams	Amount in Ounces
1/8 cup	30 g	1.1 oz.
1/4 cup	65 g	2.2 oz.
1/3 cup	85 g	2.9 oz.
3/8 cup	95 g	3.3 oz.
1/2 cup	125 g	4.4 oz.
5/8 cup	155 g	5.5 oz.
2/3 cup	165 g	5.9 oz.
3/4 cup	190 g	6.6 oz.
7/8 cup	220 g	7.7 oz.
1 cup	250 g	8.8 oz.
2 cups	500 g	17.6 oz.
4 cups	1000 g	35.3 oz.

Butter & Margarine

US Cups	Amount in Grams	Amount in Ounces
1/8 cup	28g	1 oz.
1/4 cup	57g	2 oz.
1/3 cup	75g	3 oz.
1/2 cup	113g	4 oz.
2/3 cup	150g	5 1/4 oz.
3/4 cup	170g	6 1/4 oz.
1 cup	225g	8 oz.

Conclusion

KetoFasty is a topic of great depth in itself, where a diet is brought together with a specific food consumption practice. So when a person keto fast, he gets a more directed guideline which not only can rightly prescribe the timings of the meal in a day but the type of the meal to take. Together these approaches can effectively help in garnering the essential outcomes of ketosis. This book takes this understanding to a practical standpoint where all the readers can enjoy the experience of KetoFasty right from their own kitchen floors with the help of all the delicious and variety of recipes shared in various sections. Keeping into consideration, all the very needs of the consumers, the recipes cover different meal categories. Every diet becomes more exciting when provided with delectable options, same is true with the KetoFasty. So don't miss out your chance to try some quick, easy and interesting recipes and let this book be your genuine guide in the kitchen.

Made in the USA
Lexington, KY
31 May 2019